P. Kuvc

The Divine Liturgy
of the
Holy Orthodox
Catholic
Apostolic
Graeco-Russian
Church

NIHIL SINE DEO

Author: **P. Kuvochinsky**
Editor: **Francesco Tosi**

Editio Princeps: *The Divine Liturgy of the Holy Orthodox Catholic Apostolic Graeco-Russian Church, Cope & Fenwick, 1909.*

ISBN paperback: 9781704826103

INTRODUCTORY NOTES

I.—*Of the Russian Church*

The conversion of Russia to Christianity is wholly attributable to the Greek Church. About the middle of the ninth century, when Photius was Patriarch of Constantinople, the seeds of Christianity were first sown in Russia. In the year 910 a Christian Church existed at Kieff,[1] although it had little hold upon the people of the country, who were steeped in Paganism. The establishment of the Church of Russia really dates from the year 992, when Prince Vladimir and his people accepted Christianity. Paganism was abolished. Perun, the God of Thunder, the chief of the Russian idols, was overthrown. The Court and the Boyars, and the great multitude of the people, flocked to the rivers, and in them received as a nation baptism from the Greek Bishops and Priests.[2]

1 According to tradition the Russian Church had an Apostle for its founder. St. Andrew, the first called of the Twelve, planted the first cross on the hills of Kieff. "See you," said he, to his disciples, "these hills? On these hills shall shine the light of Divine grace. There shall be a great City and God shall have in it many churches to His Name." Such are the words of the holy Nestor the Monk of the Pechersky monastery.

2 Nestor draws a graphic picture of this baptism of a whole people at once. "Some stood in the water up to their necks, others up to their breasts,

Schools were established, and churches were erected all over the country. A stone cathedral was built at Kieff, and endowed by Vladimir with a tenth part of all his revenues. Michael the Syrian was appointed Bishop of Kieff and first Metropolitan. On his death he was succeeded by Leontius, who established episcopal sees at Novgorod, Rostoff, Cheringoff, and Belgorod. Thus in an incredibly short period the Russian Church was firmly established. The conversion of Russia by the Greek Church has been described as the mightiest conquest the Christian Church has ever made since the time of the Apostles. Vladimir, "equal to the Apostles," as the people called him, was canonised as a saint and buried in the cathedral at Kieff. For six hundred years the Russian Church was ruled from Constantinople. The Russian Metropolitan, who had his place of residence at Kieff, was subject to the Patriarch of Constantinople.

In 1320 Moscow was chosen as the seat of the Metropolitan. It was not until 1589 that the Russian Church became autocephalous. In that year Job, 46th Metropolitan, was raised to the patriarchal dignity by Jeremiah, Patriarch of Constantinople— an act which was subsequently confirmed by a general council of the East. From this time forward the patriarch of the Holy Orthodox Church of Russia held a position in the country second only to that of

holding their young children in their arms; the Priests read the prayers from the shore, naming at once whole companies by their name."

the sovereign Emperor. So formidable did the power of the patriarchs become that Peter the Great in 1700 forbade the election of a new patriarch. In 1721 he, therefore, established the Holy Governing Synod to supply the place of the patriarch. This body now governs the Russian Church. The Czar is not head of the Church. All decisions in theological matters have to be given by the Synod. But the Czar has the power of appointment of all members of the Holy Synod. This body consists of five or six Bishops, one or two high ecclesiastics, and several laymen. At the head is a layman, the Chief Procurator, to represent and act in the name of Czar, by whom all decrees of the Synod must be approved before becoming law. In spite of the power thus given to the Czar in ruling the Church, he has no authority to interfere in any matter of doctrine. As has been truly said, in Russia the Church is a check on the Czar, rather than the Czar on the Church. Should the Czar change his religion he would be far more likely to lose his throne than to convert his people. Subordinate to the Holy Synod is the Consistorial Court of each Diocese (there are about seventy Dioceses in the Russian Empire). Subordinate again to the Consistorial are the Courts called Cantoirs. Appeals lie from the Cantoirs first to the Consistorial Courts, then to the Bishops, and finally to the Holy Synod.

For ecclesiastical purposes Russia is divided into eparchies of three classes, each of which is ruled over by a Bishop. There are three eparchies of the first class ruled by the Metropolitans of Kieff, Novgorod, St. Petersburg, and Moscow. In point of number of adherents the Russian Church is the largest in Christendom. It is a truly National Church in that throughout its history it has always been identified with the life of the nation. It has a tremendous hold upon the laity, who are taught to love it as part of the traditions they inherit. It presents religion in the most beautiful liturgies, through the most exalted language, and by means of the most gorgeous ceremonial.

II.—*Of the Faith of the Russian Church*

The Greek Church bases its belief on—(*a*) Holy Scripture; (*b*) The Nicene Creed; (*c*) The Seven Œcumenical Councils; (*d*) The Seven Sacraments or Mysteries. The authoritative exposition of the Faith of the Church of Russia is to be found in *the Longer and Shorter Catechisms*. These are the work of Philaret, Bishop of Moscow, and have received the sanction of the patriarchs. They were in 1839 promulgated by the Holy Governing Synod as the "Catechism of the Church herself," and have since then been in use in all the Churches and Schools of Russia. The seven Sacraments or Mysteries are—(1) Baptism, (2) Unction with Chrism, (3) The Eucharist, (4) Penance, (5) Holy Orders, (6) Marriage, (7) Unction with oil. A mystery or sacrament is defined as " a holy act through which grace, or, in other words, the saving power of God, works mysteriously upon man."

Baptism usually takes place on the eighth day after birth. The child is first exorcised to cast out the evil spirit, anointed with oil, and signed with the sign of the Cross. It is then immersed three times in the name of the Father and of the Son and of the Holy Ghost. Unction with Chrism takes the place of confirmation of the Western Church, and is conferred by a Priest with ointment consecrated by the Bishop on Thursday in Holy Week. In Russia the ointment can only be consecrated in Moscow or in Kieff. Of the Eucharist, the Longer Catechism says: " As to the *manner* in which the Bread and Wine are changed into the Body and Blood of our Lord, none but God can understand; only this much is signified, that the Bread *truly*, *really* and *substantially* becomes the very true Body of the Lord, and the Wine the very Blood of the Lord."[1] The Eucharist is administered to children after Baptism, and adults are expected to communicate four times yearly.

Unction with oil corresponds to Extreme Unction in the Western Church, with the exception that in the

[1] Following on the explanation in the Catechism comes a quotation from St. John of Damascus:—"It is truly that Body united with the Godhead, which had its origin from the Holy Virgin; not as though that Body which ascended came down from Heaven, but because the bread and wine themselves are changed into the Body and Blood of Christ. But if thou seekest after the manner how this is, let it suffice thee to be told, that it is by the Holy Ghost, in like manner as by the same Holy Ghost the Lord formed flesh to Himself and in Himself from the Mother of God; nor know I aught more than this, that the word of God is true, powerful and almighty, but in its manner of operation unsearchable."

Greek Church it is administered to the sick with a view to curing bodily, as well as spiritual, infirmities, and not as in the Roman Church solely on the point of death (in *articulo mortis*).　The Greek Church rejects the *filioque* clause in the Creed.　It also rejects the distinctively Roman doctrines of Indulgences, Purgatory, and the Immaculate Conception of the Blessed Virgin.　It teaches that there is an intermediate state, or place of expectancy for the souls of the departed until the Resurrection; that the prayers of those on earth are effective for the departed; and that the Saints should be invoked.　The Catechism says:—

Q.—How should we address ourselves in prayer to the Saints?

A.—We should ask them to pray to God for us, and by their holy prayers and entreaties to obtain from Him benefit for our souls.

While the Greek Church has never adopted the Roman doctrine of the Immaculate Conception, it pays to her the most devout homage and addresses prayers to her.　The Catechism says:—

Q.—What does the Church teach us concerning the worthiness of the most Holy Virgin Mary?

A.—It calls her by the name of Bogoroditza (God's mother), and honours her more highly than the cherubim and seraphim; that is to say, all the angelic host.

Concerning ikons in worship, the Greek Church teaches that they should be used as aids to devotion. Such as gaze on them should see, as it were, God and

the Saints who are represented. "They should be
used as devout reminders of the acts of God and of His
Saints; and, standing before them, we should pray
to God and His Saints; and, therefore, the devout
reverence that we pay should refer to the Original;
that is, to Him Who is there imaged."

III.—*Concerning the Divine Liturgies of the Russian Church*

The Church of Russia being a part of the Holy
Orthodox Catholic Apostolic Greek or Eastern Church
uses the two great Eastern liturgies—the Liturgy of
St. John Chrysostom and the Liturgy of St. Basil.[1] The
Liturgy of St. Chrysostom was written or compiled by
the holy Father whose name it bears, and, like other
liturgies, it has since received some additions and
interpolations. A tract ascribed to St. Proclus, patriarch of Constantinople, in the fifth century, refers
to the Liturgy of Chrysostom, and a translation of it
into Latin was made by Leo Thuscus in 1180. Palmer,
in his " Origines Liturgicæ," writes as follows : " Since
the Liturgy of Chrysostom professes by its name to be
the peculiar liturgy of the Church of Constantinople,
and since it has been used there and in the surround-
ing churches from time immemorial, we may
naturally expect that some notices relative to its
order and substance may be found amongst the writ-

[1] There is also the Liturgy of the Presanctified, known as The Liturgy of St.
Gregory Dialogos. It is used on Wednesdays and Fridays during Lent.

ings of the Fathers who lived in that vicinity. . . .
Severianus, Bishop of Gabala, to whom Chrysostom
entrusted the care of the Church of Constantinople
during his own absence, is said to have preached in
that city a homily on the parable of the prodigal son,
which appears among Chrysostom's works. In this
homily he speaks of several parts of the liturgy. He
notices successively the proclamation of the deacons
to the catechumens, etc., to depart out of the church,
the hymn *Tersanctus*, and the Lord's Prayer said at
the altar. Chrysostom himself, in works written
after his elevation to the patriarchal chair of Constantinople, speaks of the form *Sursum corda*, etc., of the
hymn *Tersanctus*, of the prayers or oblation for the
church, etc., and of the form *Sancta sanctis*. However few these notices may be, yet as they agree with
the substance and order of Chrysostom's liturgy, and
as no opposing testimonies seem to exist, we may
regard them as sufficient to prove that the same order
and substance of liturgy prevailed in the fourth century at Constantinople as in subsequent ages. I
would not be understood to affirm positively that the
whole text is so ancient, nor that all the rites ascend
to that century, because there is reasonable ground
for doubt with regard to certain parts; but I think
we may justly consider the main substance and order
to be as old as the fourth century. If such a form of
liturgy was used at Constantinople in the fourth
century, it is very probable that it may have been
used also in the neighbouring churches. In fact, we

find that all the churches of Thrace, Macedonia and Greece have from time immemorial used this very Liturgy of Chrysostom."

St. Basil, Archbishop of Cæsarea in Cappadocia, is supposed to have been the first to compile a liturgy *in writing* for the use of his own church. The exarchate or patriarchate of Cæsarea extended from the Hellespont to the Euphrates, and with the exception of the pro-consular Asia, Phrygia, and some maritime provinces, included the whole of Asia Minor. Cæsarea in Cappadocia was the metropolis of the exarchate, and Basil, commonly called " the Great," was consecrated bishop of Cæsarea about 370 A.D. In the Russian Church the Liturgy of St. Basil is used upon all Sundays in Lent except Palm Sunday, upon Maundy Thursday and Easter eve, upon the vigils of Christmas and the Epiphany, also on St. Basil's day, January 1. At other times the Liturgy of St. Chrysostom is used. The Liturgy of St. Basil differs from that of St. John Chrysostom only in certain of the prayers recited secretly by the Priest, in one Hymn, and three phrases in the Consecration of the Holy Gifts. The Liturgy of St. Chrysostom is, in fact, a later and abbreviated form of St. Basil's Liturgy, just as St. Basil's Liturgy is a later and abbreviated form of some still earlier liturgy—of Apostolic origin. Both liturgies consist of three distinct parts. The first part, during which the priest prepares the sacred bread and wine ready for consecration, is known as *The Office of Oblation.* The second part, consisting of prayers, reading, and singing in preparation for the Holy Sacrifice, is known as the *Liturgy of the Catechumens.* It ends with the dismissal of the Catechumens by the Deacon in these words: "Depart all ye Catechumens, depart. Let all the Catechumens depart. Let no Catechumen remain." The third part, known as the *Liturgy of the Faithful,* consists of the celebration of the Holy Mysteries. It has these four features: the Great Eucharistic Prayer, the Consecration, the Intercession for quick and dead, and the Communion.

The form of Consecration is worth attention. It consists of the Words of Institution for the Bread, "This is My Body," etc.; the Words of Institution for the Wine; the Oblation of the Precious Gifts; Prayer for the Descent of the Holy Ghost; Prayer for the Change of Elements. This prayer for the descent of the Holy Ghost is a distinctive feature of all Eastern Liturgies, and is undoubtedly primitive. It is not to be found in the Roman Mass. The Roman Church holds that the *whole Consecration* of the elements consists in the words, *This is My Body; This is My Blood.*

The Eastern Church holds that three things are necessary for the Consecration: (1) The recitation of the words of Institution; (2) The Oblation of the Elements; (3) The Invocation of the Holy Ghost. The words in the Liturgy of St. John Chrysostom are these: *Make this Bread the precious Blood of Thy Christ, and that which is in this Cup the precious Blood of Thy Christ, changing them by Thy Holy Spirit.*

IV.— *Of the Arrangement of a Russian Church*

Every Russian Church consists of four portions.

(1) The Sanctuary or Altar beyond the Image Screen (ikonostasis).

(2) The Choir, which consists of two parts (a) the Tribune immediately in front of the Holy Door in the centre of the screen (b) the railed places for the choirs on either side of the Tribune.

(3) The Nave.

(4) The Western Porch.

The building is usually in the form of a ship or of a cross. North of the altar—there is only one altar[1] in every Russian Church—is the Chapel of Oblation with credence table, at which the preparation of the Elements takes place. At the back of the Holy Table is a representation of the Crucifixion, before which stands a lamp with seven branches. A Pyx containing the reserved Sacrament stands upon the Holy Table, a lighted lamp suspended before it. On the Table itself lies a Book of the Gospel and a Cross. Behind the altar is the High Place, an elevation upon which stands the Bishop's throne. South of the Sanctuary is the sacristy. The Sanctuary is separated from the choir by a solid screen, on which are the ikons. Three doors give access

1 The name "Altar" is not always applied merely to the Holy Table, but often is used to signify the whole space between it and the ikonostasis. In this work, however, the familiar term "the altar" has frequently been used to denote simply "the Holy Table."

through it, the centre one to the altar, another to the table of oblation, and the third to the Sanctuary. The central opening is known as the Holy Door. Through it no unordained person may pass at any time. Inside the Holy Door is a curtain which is drawn or withdrawn at various times during Divine service. Outside on the right of the Holy Door is the ikon of the Saviour, next to it is the ikon of the Patron Saint of the particular church. On the left is the ikon of the Blessed Virgin, while on the leaves of the Holy Door itself are the ikons of the four Evangelists together with a representation of the Annunciation. Over the Holy Door is an ikon of the Last Supper. On the north and south and doors are ikons of angels or of holy Deacons. In the nave the men are placed on the right and the women on the left. They generally stand or kneel throughout the service—these two attitudes being the only ones recognised as fitting for worshippers. Lights are always used during divine service. Behind the altar is a seven-branched candlestick, and upon the altar itself are tapers. At Pontifical services are placed upon the altar the double and triple-branched candlesticks wherewith the Bishop bestows his blessing on the congregation,

Of special sacred vessels and implements not in use in the Western Church mention may be made of the following:—

The Asterisk.—Made of two large thin pieces of silver or other metal in the form of an arch, and crossing each other in the middle. It supports the Veil above the paten so that it may not touch the Holy Body. Its mystical meaning is the star which led the Wise Men to the Infant Saviour.

The Spear.—With which the particles are taken from the Altar-breads.

The Spoon.—All persons, both infants and adults, are communicated with the Holy Body and Blood by the sacred spoon.

The Air.—A large linen cloth with which both Paten and Chalice are covered. It is called the "air" because as the air surrounds the earth, so does this surround the holy gifts.

The Sacramental Fans.—Represent the six-winged Seraphim. With them the Holy Elements are fanned to keep off flies and insects. The fans are now generally made of silver.

V.— *Of the Vestments worn by the Ministers of the Russian Church*

The Sacerdotal vestments worn by the Ministers of the Russian Church differ slightly from those worn by the Ministers of the Western Church. The distinctive vestment of the Russian Priest is the chasuble, a sleeveless garment, long at the back but short in front, with an opening for the head. The stole is different from that of the West, being merely a long piece of silk or stuff about double the width of a Western stole, and with a hole in the middle of the upper part through which the Priest puts his head.

B

When serving at the altar the priest wears a zone or girdle above his cassock and stole and gauntlets on his wrists. A Bishop wears all the vestments of a priest except the chasuble. In place of this he wears a wide-sleeved dalmatic without a seam woven from top to bottom. His stole, called an omophorion, resembles the Latin *pallium*, and is very broad and hangs down in front and behind over his other vestments. The Bishop's mantle is a monastic vestment of purple. Its colour is, as a rule, purple, and upon it are sewn the "Tables of the Law," and red and white buttons known as "Fountains." The Mitre is of a different shape to that worn in the West. The Pectoral Image worn on a Bishop's breast is generally a small circular ikon of our Lord or of the Blessed Virgin. During divine service the Bishop stands upon a circular rug known as the "eagle," so called on account of it bearing a picture representing an eagle soaring over a city. The city signifies the diocese of the Bishop; and the eagle is in allusion to St. John the Divine being represented in pictures with that bird.

The Deacon who takes such a prominent part in all Eastern liturgies is vested in a long dalmatic with wide sleeves. His stole, called an Orarium, is a long wide band of silk which is worn sometimes over his left shoulder and sometimes crossed upon his breast. He also wears gauntlets for convenience during the service of the Altar. The vestments are made of gold and silver cloth, of brocade or silk material, varying

in richness according to the means of the particular
church.   In an ordinary parish they are made of
brocade, and for special high days and holy days,
such as Christmas, Easter, the Emperor's name day,
the 30th August, the Feast of St. Alexander Neffsky,
a great Russian Saint, the Ascension to the Throne,
etc., of white silver cloth.   For Lent, funerals and
requiems black velvet vestments, trimmed with
silver lace, are used.

VI.—*Of the Symbolical Significance of the Liturgies*

Every action of the Priest and every vessel used
in Divine Service have a symbolical significance.
"The wax which we offer and burn," says Simion
Sobounsky, "being the purest of materials, signifies
the purity and sincerity of our offering; as a material
which is capable of impression, it typifies the seal or
sign of the Cross made on us at Baptism and Unction;
as a soft and yielding material, it represents our
obedience and willingness to repent; wax, collected
as it is from the most fragrant flowers, signifies the
Grace of the Holy Spirit."

The bread used for the Eucharist is of the finest
wheaten flour, worked with yeast and salted.   The
flour and yeast signify our souls, the water Baptism,
and the salt wisdom and the teaching of the Word.
The bread is made into little loaves of about three
ounces weight, and is formed of two pieces (typical
of the twofold nature of Christ).   The upper part of
the loaf is smaller than the lower part, and the top is

stamped with a seal bearing the impression of a cross and a Slavonic cypher, signifying "Jesus Christ the Conqueror." Though the Eucharist may consist of morsels taken from one loaf only, it is the general custom to use five, in remembrance of the miracle of the five loaves (St. John vi. 9-15).

The preparation of the bread and wine for the celebration is full of symbolical significance. The Priest, taking the first loaf and making the sign of the cross over it with the spear, cuts it right and left, bringing away the stamped portion known as the Lamb. He then pierces the Lamb on the right side, symbolising the soldiers who pierced the Saviour's side with a spear as He hung upon the Cross. From the second loaf a three-cornered portion is cut out in honour and remembrance of the Blessed Virgin, and is placed to the right side of the Lamb on the paten. "Upon Thy right hand did stand the Queen in gold of Ophir" (Psalm xlv. 9).

From the third loaf nine pieces are cut out in honour of (1) the Prophet Forerunner and Baptist St. John, (2) The rest of the Prophets, (3) St. Peter and St. Paul and the rest of the Apostles, (4) The Fathers and Bishops of the Church, (5) The Martyrs, (6) Holy men and women, (7) The ascetics and those who have made themselves "beggars" for Christ's sake, (8) St. Joachim and Anna, the parents of the Blessed Virgin, and the Saints of the Day, (9) St. John Chrysostom or St. Basil (according to the Liturgy used). These pieces are placed on the left side of the Lamb.

From the fourth loaf pieces are cut with prayer for the living—the Episcopate, the Bishop of the Diocese, the priesthood, the Czar, etc. From the fifth pieces are cut with prayer for the repose of departed Bishops, the founders of the Church in which the service is being performed, and others by name. Anyone who wishes can have a friend, either dead or living, commemorated by application to the priest before the service. Two lists of names are prepared, one of the living and one of the dead, and as the Priest reads over these lists at every name a particle of the bread is set apart as their particular portion. Last of all, the Priest cuts out a piece for himself. All these pieces are arranged round the Lamb in allusion to St. John xvii. 24.

There are three veils, or coverings, made of damask, velvet, or cloth of gold, embroidered and ornamented in various manners. The two smaller veils are used to cover the cup and paten, and represent the swaddling clothes of the infant Jesus. The third, called the Air (see Note IV.), signifies the linen cloth mentioned in Scripture, Matthew xxvii. 59 ("And when Joseph had taken the body, he wrapped it in a clean linen cloth ").

The commencement of the second part of the Liturgy—the Liturgy of the Catechumens—is signalised by the drawing aside of the curtain from behind the Holy Door. The curtain represents the Tabernacle in Heaven before God, where the holy angels and the saints of God dwell. At the procession of the

Lesser Entrance the Priest comes forth, followed by the Deacon, who carries a large book of the Gospels, typifying the teaching and preaching of our Lord. They are preceded by the Reader carrying a lighted taper, typical of John the Baptist and the prophets who preached of His coming, and also symbolical of the light of the Gospel.

The Great Entrance—the carrying of the Elements from the Prothesis (or Table of Oblation) to the Altar—is the most imposing ceremony in the Russian Church. It symbolises the last Advent of Christ when he shall come with glory. First comes the Reader bearing a high candlestick with a lighted candle. After this follow the Deacon or Deacons in order symbolising the ranks of angels. Then come those who bear the Holy Gifts. If there be more than one present, each of the rest holds a sacred object —the cross, the spoon, the spear. The veil is kept over the holy gifts until the Creed is finished, in token that we must first make a true confession about our Lord before we can behold Him without any veil. At the final preparation of the Eucharist for communion and the reception by the clergy the curtain is drawn over the Holy Door to call to remembrance the burial of Christ and His sojourn in the tomb. The elevation of the Bread sets forth to us the elevation of Jesus on the Cross. When the Priest breaks the Holy Bread into four pieces and taking the upper portion places it in the chalice, it is symbolical of the union of Body and Blood of Christ. The addition of warm

water to the chalice signifies the returning to life of
His most pure Body at his Divine Resurrection. St.
Germanus explains as follows :—" As Blood and warm
water flowed both of them from the side of Christ,
thus hot water poured into the chalice at the time of
consecration gives a full type of the mystery to those
who draw that Holy Liquid from the chalice, as from
the life-giving side of our Lord." At the communion
of the congregation the Holy Door is opened, typical
of the miraculous opening of the Holy Sepulchre, and
the Deacon, holding the Cup in his two hands on a
level with his face, invites the people to approach.
He then hands the Cup to the Priest, who, taking a
morsel of the Bread in the Spoon with a little Wine,
puts it in the mouth of the communicant. The
Deacon holds a veil beneath the chin of the communicant to prevent the possibility of a drop falling to the
ground, and wipes his lips with it afterwards. The
communicant then kisses the edge of the Cup and
makes the sign of the cross. Children and babies in
arms also receive the sacrament in like manner. The
use of the Spoon for administration of the Blessed
Sacrament was established by St. John Chrysostom.
Until his time men used to receive the bread in their
hands, and the women on a handkerchief; but the
following act of sacrilege induced St. John Chrysostom to abolish this practice: A woman, having
received the Body of Christ, took It home with her,
and mingled It with a charm for witchcraft. When
this became known to Chrysostom he ordained that

the Body should no longer be given into the hands of the laity, but be put into their mouths by the priest by means of a spoon, together with the sacred Blood.

After he has received, the communicant goes up to a little table, where the Reader stands with a ladle full of warm water and wine, intended as a sort of rinsing after the Eucharist and the Antidoron—the bread which has been offered for the service of the Altar, but which has not been required for consecration. To this bread a particular sanctity attaches, and in Russia the most austere monks frequently make the Antidoron their sole food during Lent.

THE LITURGIES

OF

St. JOHN CHRYSOSTOM

AND OF

St. BASIL THE GREAT

I. THE OFFICE OF OBLATION

The Priest, having entered the Temple, shall bow three times in company with the Deacon before the Holy Door. Then the Deacon shall say:

Master, give the blessing.

The Priest:

Blessed be our God at all times, now and ever, world without end. Amen.

The Deacon:

O King of Heaven, Comforter, Spirit of Truth, Who art in all places and endureth all things; Fountain of all good, and Giver of Life; Abide in our hearts, and cleanse us from every stain; save our souls, O beneficent One.

O Holy One, Holy omnipotent and ever living God, have mercy upon us. *(Thrice.)*

Glory be to the Father, and to the Son, and to the Holy Ghost, now and ever, world without end. Amen.

O most Holy Trinity have mercy upon us. O Lord wash away our sins. O Master pardon our offences, O Holy One look mercifully upon our infirmities and heal them for Thy Name's sake.

Lord, have mercy upon us. *(Thrice.)*

Our Father Who art in Heaven, Hallowed be Thy Name. Thy Kingdom come. Thy will be done on earth, as it is in Heaven. Give us this day our daily bread, and forgive us our trespasses, as we forgive them that trespass against us. And lead us not into temptation. But deliver us from evil.

The Priest:

For Thine is the kingdom, the power and the glory of the Father and the Son and the Holy Ghost, now and ever, world without end. Amen.

Then shall they say:

Have mercy upon us, O God. Have mercy upon us. For inasmuch as we sinners are without defence, we offer to Thee, our Master, this supplication; have mercy upon us. Glory be to the Father and to the Son and to the Holy Ghost. Have mercy upon us, O

Lord; for in Thee have we put our trust; and be not wrath with us, neither remember our transgressions; but look down upon us in Thy tender compassion and deliver us from our enemies, for Thou art our God, and we are Thy people, and the works of Thy hand, and we call upon Thy name, now and ever, world without end. Amen.

And this Hymn to the Mother of God:

Open unto us the door of thy loving kindness, O blessed Mother of God; we have set our hope on Thee, may we be not disappointed, but through Thee may we be delivered from adversity, for Thou art the saving help of all Christian people.

Then approaching the Ikon of Christ, they shall kiss it and sing:

To Thy pure image, O Beneficent One, we do homage, entreating pardon for our sins, O Christ our God; for of Thine own goodwill Thou wert graciously pleased to ascend the Cross as very Man, that Thou mightest deliver from the bonds of the enemy those whom Thou hadst created; therefore do we lift up our souls to Thee and give thanks.

Then shall they kiss the Ikon of the Mother of God, and recite the following hymn in a low voice·

O, Mother of God, Thou Who art a deep well of

infinite mercy, bestow upon us Thy compassion; look upon Thy people who have sinned, and continue to make manifest Thy power. For Thee do we trust, and to Thee we cry Hail, even as of old did Gabriel, the chief of the angelic hosts.

With bowed heads they then say the following prayer:

Stretch forth Thy hand, O Lord, from Thy Holy habitation on high, and grant me strength for this Thine appointed service, so that standing absolved before Thy dread altar I may administer the sacred bloodless rite, for Thine is the power throughout all ages. Amen.

Then making a reverence to the people, they enter the Sanctuary, and say in a low voice:

I will enter into Thy house, I will bow toward Thy Holy Temple in Thy fear. Guide me, O Lord with Thy perfection, make straight my path because of mine enemies, for there is no truth in their mouth, their heart is vanity, their throat is an open sepulchre, and they speak falsely with their tongues. Judge them, O Lord, and let them perish through their own counsels; cast them out according to the multitude of their iniquities, for they have provoked Thee exceedingly, O Lord. And let all those who put their trust in Thee be joyful, so shall they be filled with gladness evermore; for Thou shalt dwell amongst them for ever; and they who love Thy name shall make their boast in Thee; for Thou, O Lord, will bless the righteous And Thou hast covered us with the panoply of Thy approbation.

Upon entering the Sanctuary they bow three times before the Altar, and kissing the Book of the Gospels and the Holy Table say:

O Lord, purify Thou me a sinner.

Then the Deacon shall draw near to the Priest, holding in his right hand his Dalmatic, Stole and Gauntlets, and bowing his head before the Priest shall say:

Bless, Master, this Dalmatic and this Stole.

The Priest:

Blessed is our God, always, now and ever, world without end. Amen.

Then the Deacon shall retire, and having kissed the Cross on his Dalmatic, shall robe himself therein, and shall say the following prayer:

My soul shall rejoice in the Lord, for He hath put upon me the robe of salvation, and has clothed me with the garment of gladness. He hath set a crown upon my head, like unto a bridegroom; and as a bride has adorned me with comeliness.

Then having kissed the Stole, he shall lay it upon his right shoulder, and putting the Gauntlet upon his right wrist shall say:

Thy right hand, O Lord, is glorified in strength; Thy right hand, O Lord, hath broken the adversary; and through the greatness of Thy glory hast Thou destroyed Thine enemy.

And putting a second Gauntlet upon his left wrist he shall say:

Thy hands have made me and fashioned me; enlighten my understanding that I may learn Thy commandments.

Then going to the Table of Oblation, he shall prepare the Holy Things; the Paten he shall set upon the left side, the Chalice upon the right side. Then shall the Priest take his Dalmatic in his left hand, and bowing three times towards the East he shall sign it with the sign of the Cross, and say:

Blessed is our God always, now and ever, world without end. Amen.

My soul shall rejoice in the Lord, for He hath put upon me the robe of salvation, and has clothed me with the garment of gladness. He hath set a crown upon my head, like unto a bridegroom; and as a bride has adorned me with comeliness.

Then taking the Stole he shall sign it with the sign of the Cross, and placing it upon his shoulders shall say:

Blessed is God who poureth forth upon His priests His grace, like unto the precious ointment upon the head of Aaron, which ran down upon his beard, and even to the skirts of his clothing.

Then shall he take the Girdle, and girding himself shall say:

Blessed is God Who girdeth me with strength, and hath freed my path from blame, and made my feet like unto those of an hart, and set me on high.

Then shall he put the Gauntlets upon his wrists in the same manner as appointed for the Deacon, and taking his Epigonation, if he possess the dignity, he shall bless it, saying:*

Gird Thy sword upon Thy thigh, O mighty One, in Thy vigour and beauty. Go forth and prosper, and rule in truth and humility and goodness; and may Thy right hand guide Thee wondrously at all times, now and ever, world without end. Amen.

* The Epigonation is an oblong piece of brocade which is suspended upon the hip of a priest, it signifies the Sword of the Spirit which is the Word of God. It is also explained as being symbolical of the towel wherewith Our Lord washed His disciples' feet.

Then shall he take the Chasuble and bless it, and having kissed it shall put it upon him, saying:

Thy priests, O Lord, shall clothe themselves in righteousness, and Thy holy ones shall rejoice in triumph at all times, now and ever, world without end. Amen.

Then shall they wash their hands, saying:

I will wash my hands in innocency, O Lord, and so will I go to Thine altar, that I may hear the voice of Thy praise and tell of Thy wondrous works. Lord, I have loved the beauty of Thy house and the place wherein Thy glory dwelleth.   Destroy not my soul with the ungodly, nor my life with the men of blood, in whose hands is wickedness, though their right hand be full of gifts. But as for me, I will walk in innocence.   O deliver me, Lord, and have mercy upon me; my foot standeth on righteousness.   In the congregations will I praise Thee, O Lord.

Then they go forth to the Chapel of Oblation, making three lowly reverences before the Holy Table, and all shall say privately:

O God, cleanse Thou me a sinner, and have mercy upon me. By Thy precious blood hast Thou redeemest us from the judgment of the Lord, for Thou wert nailed to the Cross and pierced with the spear.

Upon mankind hast Thou poured immortality as from a fountain, O Redeemer. Glory be to Thee.

The Hours are now read while the Bread and Wine are prepared for the Sacrament.

The Deacon (in a loud voice):

Master, give the blessing.

The Priest:

Blessed be our God at all times, now and ever, world without end.

The Deacon:

Amen.

Then the Priest shall take the Breads* into his left hand, and holding in his right the Holy Spear shall make therewith thrice the sign of the Cross above the seal on the Bread, saying:

In remembrance of our God and Saviour the Lord Jesus Christ. *(Thrice.)*

---

* Five loaves are provided in the Chapel of Oblation, in commemoration of the miracle of the five loaves. They are small round loaves with a square seal or projection stamped upon them in the centre. This seal or projection is the part of the bread known as the Holy Lamb.

c

And immediately he shall thrust the Spear into the right side of the Seal, and as he pierceth it shall say:

He was led as a sheep to the slaughter.

And piercing the left shall say:

And as a spotless lamb before his shearers is dumb, so opened He not His lips.

And piercing the top shall say:

In His humiliation His judgment was taken away.

And piercing it from underneath shall say:

For His generation who shall declare it?

And the Deacon, gazing reverently at the Mystic Rite, holding his Stole in his hand, shall say at each incision:

Let us pray to the Lord.

While the Priest thrusts the Spear obliquely from below into the right side of the Bread, and removes the part upon which is imprinted the Seal, the Deacon shall say:

Master, take it hence, for This Life is taken from the earth.

The Priest having laid it inverted upon the Paten, and the Deacon having said:

Master, make the Sacrifice.

He shall sacrifice it, cutting it crosswise, and say:

Sacrificed is the Lamb of God who taketh away the sins of the world, for the life of the world and its salvation.

He shall then turn upward the other side, which beareth upon it the emblem of the Cross, and shall pierce the right side with the Spear, while the Deacon shall say:

Pierce, Master.

And the Priest shall say:

One of the soldiers pierced His side with a spear and there came forth blood and water. And he that saw it bare witness, and his witness is true.

Then the Deacon shall pour into the Chalice the Wine and the Water, saying:

Bless, Master, this Holy Union.

And the Priest shall bless it, saying:

Blessed be the Union of these Holy Things, at all times, now and ever, world without end. Amen.

Then he shall take in his hand another Bread, and shall say:

In honour and commemoration of our most Blessed Lady Mary, Mother of God and Ever-Virgin, through Whose intercession, we beseech Thee, O God, to accept this Sacrifice upon Thy most Heavenly Altar.

And taking out a portion with the Spear, he shall lay it on the right side of the Holy Bread, saying:

On Thy right hand stood the Queen Mother in a garment wrought about with gold and divers colours.

Then taking a third Bread, he shall say:

In commemoration of the most venerable and glorious prophet John the Baptist who foretold Thy coming.

Then taking the first Particle he shall place it on the left hand of the Holy Bread, making the beginning of the first row, and shall say:

Of the Holy Glorious Prophets Moses and Aaron, Elijah and Elisha, David and Jesse, of the Three Holy Children, and of Daniel the Prophet, and of all the Holy Prophets.

*Then taking another Particle, he shall place it below the
first and say:*

Of the holy glorious and most laudable Apostles
Peter and Paul, and of the other holy Apostles.

*In the same manner he shall place a third Particle below
the second, thus completing the first line, and shall say:*

Of our holy fathers and saints the Prelates Basil
the Great, Gregory the Doctor, and St. John Chry-
sostom; Athanasius and Cyril, Nicholas of Myra in
Lycia; Peter, Alexis, Jonah, and Philip of Moscow,
Nikíta Bishop of Novgorod, Leóntieff Bishop of
Rostóff, and of all Thy holy Prelates.

*Then taking out a fourth Particle, he shall place it beside
the first Particle, making a beginning of the second line,
and shall say:*

Of the Holy Apostle and first Martyr and Arch-
deacon Stephen; of the great and Holy Martyrs
Dimetrius, George, Theodore of Tyre, Theodore the
Strategian, and of all holy Martyrs both men and
women; of Thekla, Barbara, Euphemia, Kyriaka,
Paraskeva, Katherine, and of all other holy women
who suffered martyrdom.

*Then taking out a fifth Particle, he shall place it beside
the first of the second line, and shall say:*

Of our devout and pious Fathers Anthony,

Uthymius, Sabbas, Onuphrius, Athanasius of Mount Athos, Anthony and Theodosius of the Catacombs, Sergius of Radónezh, Barlaam of Khútinsk, and of all our saintly Fathers; and of our saintly mothers in God, Pelagia, Theodosia, Anastasia, Euprasia, Fevronia, Theodulia, Euphrosyne, Mary of Egypt; and of all our holy and saintly mothers.

Then taking out a sixth Particle, he shall place it beside the second, completing the second line, and shall say:

Of the holy self-effacing miracle workers Cosmas and Damian, Cyrus and John, Panteliemon, Hermolaus, and of all the holy ascetics.

Then taking out a seventh Particle, he shall place it below the first of the second line, making the beginning of the third line, and shall say:

Of the holy and righteous ancestors of God, Joachim and Anna. And of Saint N. *(the Saint of the day);* and of Saint Methodius and Saint Cyril, the equal of the Apostles; and of all the Saints through whose supplications we beseech Thee to visit us, O Lord.

Then taking out an eighth Particle, he shall place it below the second of the second line, and shall say:

Of our Father in the Saints John Chrysostom,

Archbishop of Constantinople *(if his Liturgy is to be celebrated. But if the Liturgy of St. Basil the Great is to be celebrated his name shall be commemorated instead).*

Then taking out the ninth Particle, he shall place it at the end of the third line, thus completing it, and taking the fourth Bread up, he shall say:

Remember, O Lord, Cherisher of mankind, every orthodox bishopric; the Most Holy governing Synod, and all orthodox Patriarchs; and our Bishop *(here insert name);* the most honourable priesthood, the Diaconate of Christ, and every Sacredotal Order; our brethren and fellow ministers, the priests, deacons, and all our brethren whom Thou hast brought into Thy communion through Thy loving kindness, O beneficent God.

And taking out a portion, he shall lay it below the Holy Bread, and shall commemorate the Emperor, saying:

Remember, O Lord, our most God-fearing Sovereign N. Emperor of all the Russias and all the reigning house.

Then he shall make mention by name of any living persons who are to be prayed for, and at each name he shall take out a Particle, saying:

Remember, O Lord. N.

Having thus taken out the Particles, the Priest shall place them below the Holy Bread, and taking the fifth Bread shall say:

In memory and for the remission of sins of the most holy Patriarchs of the Orthodox and God-fearing Czars and Czaritzas; and of the blessed founders of this holy Church.

Then he shall make mention by name of the Bishop who ordained him, and of whatsoever persons who have departed this life he may think fit. At each name he shall take out a Particle, saying:

Remember O Lord, N.

Then he shall say as follows:

And of all our Orthodox Fathers and Brethren who have fallen asleep in the hope of resurrection, of life eternal, and of Communion with Thee, O Lord, Thou Cherisher of mankind.

Then he shall take out a Particle, and shall say:

Remember, O Lord, my unworthiness, and pardon my transgressions whether voluntary or involuntary.

Then he shall take from the fourth Bread a Particle, and with the sponge shall gather the Particles taken from the fourth and fifth Breads, on to the Paten, that they may be in safety, and that none of them may fall.   Then the Deacon shall take the Censer, place incense thereon, and say to the Priest:

Master, bless the Censer.

And the Priest shall say:

Let us pray to the Lord.

And then the prayer of the Censer:

Unto Thee, O Christ our God, we offer incense, the symbol of spiritual fragrance; be pleased to accept it upon Thy Heavenly Altar, and in its stead vouchsafe to us the grace of Thine all Holy Spirit.

The Deacon:

Let us pray to the Lord.

Then the Priest shall cense the Asterisk or Star-Cover, and placing it over the Holy Bread shall say:

The Star came and stood over the place where the Young Child was.

The Deacon:

Let us pray to the Lord.

The Priest shall then cense the first Veil and cover therewith the Holy Bread, and say:

The Lord is King and hath put on glorious apparel: the Lord hath put on his apparel, and girded himself with strength.

He hath made the round world so sure: that it cannot be moved.

Ever since the word began hath thy seat been prepared: thou art from everlasting.

The floods are risen, O Lord, the floods have lift up their voice: the floods lift up their waves.

The waves of the sea are mighty, and rage horribly: but yet the Lord, who dwelleth on high, is mightier.

Thy testimonies, O Lord, are very sure: holiness becometh thine house for ever.

The Deacon:

Let us pray to the Lord.

Cover Master.

The Priest shall cense the second Veil and shall cover therewith the Chalice, and say:

Shelter us with the covering of Thy Wings, and drive away from us our enemies, and those that hate us. Give peace in our time, O Lord; have mercy upon us and upon all Thy people; save our souls for Thou only art good, and lovest mankind.

Then the Priest shall take the cover, cense the Table of Oblation, and say thrice:

Blessed art Thou, O our God, and in this art Thou well pleased.   Glory be to Thee.

And each time the Deacon shall respond:

Always now and ever world without end.   Amen.

Then both shall bow devoutly three times, and the Deacon shall take the Censer and say:

For the precious gifts now offered up let us thank the Lord.

Then the Priest shall make the prayer of Oblation:

O God our God, who didst send forth the Heavenly Bread, the life of the whole world, our Lord and God Jesus Christ to be our Saviour, our Redeemer and Benefactor, and to bless and to sanctify us; be pleased to bless this oblation and to accept it upon Thy Heavenly Altar.   Remember of Thy great goodness and love those who offer it, and those for whom it is offered   And preserve us without blame in the celebration of Thy Divine Mysteries.   Blessed and glorified be the most noble and majestic Name of the Father and the Son and of the Holy Ghost now and ever world without end.   Amen.

Then shall the Priest pronounce the dismissal, saying:

Glory to Thee, O Christ our God and Hope. Glory to Thee.

The Deacon:

Glory be to the Father and to the Son and to the Holy Ghost, now and ever world without end. Amen.
Lord have mercy *(thrice).*
Master, give the blessing.

Then the Priest shall pronounce the benediction:

(If it be Sunday) May He Who rose from the dead, Christ our True God *[See Benediction on page 140.]*
(But on other days) May Christ our true God, through the intercession of His undefiled Mother, of our Father among the Saints John Chrysostom, Archbishop of Constantinople; *(or if the Liturgy of St. Basil be used)* of St. Basil the Great, of Caesarea in Cappadocia, and of all the Saints, have mercy upon us and save us; for He is good and loveth mankind.

The Deacon:

Amen.

After the Benediction the Deacon shall cense the Holy Oblation, and the Holy Water round about in the form of a Cross, saying in a low voice:

Thou didst enter the grave with the body, but

didst descend into Hell with the soul; for Thou art Very God; Thou wert in Paradise with the thief, and on the throne with the Father and the Holy Ghost. O Christ Who filleth all things in Thine Infinity.

Then he shall say this Psalm:

Have mercy upon me, O God, after Thy great goodness: according to the multitude of Thy mercies do away mine offences.

Wash me throughly from my wickedness: and cleanse me from my sin.

For I acknowledge my faults: and my sin is ever before me.

Against Thee only have I sinned, and done this evil in Thy sight: that Thou mightest be justified in Thy saying, and clear when Thou art judged.

Behold, I was shapen in wickedness: and in sin hath my mother conceived me.

But lo, Thou requireth truth in the inward parts: Thou shalt make me to understand wisdom secretly.

Thou shalt purge me with hyssop, and I shall be clean: Thou shalt wash me, and I shall be whiter than snow.

Thou shalt make me hear of joy and gladness: that the bones which Thou hast broken may rejoice.

Turn Thy face from my sins: and put out all my misdeeds.

Make me a clean heart, O God: and renew a right spirit within me.

Cast me not from Thy presence : and take not Thy Holy Spirit from me.

O give me the comfort of Thy help again : and establish me with Thy free Spirit.

Then shall I teach Thy ways unto the wicked : and sinners shall be converted unto Thee.

Deliver me from blood-guiltiness, O God, Thou art the God of my health : and my tongue shall sing of righteousness.

Thou shalt open my lips, O Lord : and my mouth shall shew Thy praise.

For Thou desirest no sacrifice, else would I give it Thee : but Thou delightest not in burnt offerings.

The sacrifice of God is a troubled spirit : a broken and contrite heart, O God, shalt thou not despise.

O be favourable and gracious unto Sion : build Thou the walls of Jerusalem.

Then shalt Thou be pleased with the sacrifice of righteousness, with the burnt-offerings and oblations : then shall they offer young bullocks upon Thine Altar.

While he reciteth he shall cense the Sanctuary and all the Temple, and then return again to the Holy Altar; and having again censed it, and the Priest, he shall lay the Censer in its appointed place, and draw near to the Priest. Then together before the Altar they shall bow three times, saying in a low voice :

O Heavenly King, the Comforter, Spirit of Truth

Who art in all places and in all things. Treasury of all good and Giver of life, abide in us and cleanse us from every stain; save our souls O Benefactor. Glory to God in the highest, and on earth peace and good-will towards men *(Twice)*. O Lord, open my lips, and my mouth shall show forth Thy praise.

Then the Priest shall kiss the Book of the Gospels, and the Deacon shall kiss the Altar. Then the Deacon, bowing his head before the Priest and holding his Stole with the first three fingers of his left hand, shall say:

It is time to sacrifice unto the Lord. Master, give the blessing.

And the Priest, signing him with the sign of the Cross, shall say:

Blessed is our God at all times, now and ever world without end.

The Deacon:

Pray for me, Holy Master.

The Priest:

May the Lord direct thy steps into every good work.

The Deacon:

Remember me, Holy Master.

The Priest:

May the Lord God remember Thee in His kingdom at all times, now and ever, world without end.

The Deacon:

Amen.

Then having made a genuflection, he shall go out through the north door, and standing before the Holy Door he shall bow his head devoutly, saying:

O Lord, open Thou my lips, and my mouth shall show forth Thy praise.

THE DIVINE LITURGY

II. THE LITURGY OF THE CATECHUMENS

The Deacon:

Master, give the blessing.

The Priest on the topmost step of the Altar bestoweth the blessing crosswise with the Book of the Gospels, and says:

Blessed be the Kingdom of the Father and of the Son and of the Holy Ghost, now and ever, world without end.

The Choir:

Amen.

And if it be at Eastertide:

Christ is risen from the dead, conquering death by death, and bestowing life upon those within the grave.

D

The Deacon:

In peace let us make our supplications to the Lord.

The Choir:

Lord have mercy.

The Deacon:

For the peace that is from above and for the salvation of our souls let us make our supplications to the Lord.

The Choir:

Lord, have mercy.

The Deacon:

For the peace of the whole world, the stability of the Holy Churches of God, and for the unity of all, let us make our supplications to the Lord.

The Choir:

Lord, have mercy.

The Deacon:

For this holy house, and for those that in faith, piety and the fear of God do enter therein, let us make our supplications to the Lord.

The Choir:

Lord, have mercy.

The Deacon:

For our Holy Synod, for our Archbishop N., for the venerable Priesthood, for the Diaconate in Christ, and for all the Clergy and the Laity, let us make our supplications to the Lord.

The Choir:

Lord, have mercy.

The Deacon:

For our most pious and divinely preserved Emperor, for his Consort the most religious N., for his heir the orthodox N., and all the reigning house, and for his army, let us make our supplications to the Lord.

The Choir:

Lord, have mercy.

The Deacon:

That He may fight upon their side, and subdue all their enemies and adversaries under their feet, let us make our supplications to the Lord.

The Choir:

Lord, have mercy.

The Deacon:

For this town and for every city and country, and for those who in Faith dwell therein, let us make supplications to the Lord.

The Choir:

Lord, have mercy.

The Deacon:

For healthful seasons, abundance of the fruits of the earth, and for peaceful days, let us make our supplications to the Lord.

The Choir:

Lord, have mercy.

The Deacon:

For those that travel, or journey, for those that are sick, that labour, for those that are in bonds and for their safety, let us make supplications to the Lord.

The Choir:

Lord, have mercy.

The Deacon:

That we may be preserved from all tribulation, wrath, danger, and necessity, let us make our supplications to the lord.

The Choir:

Lord, have mercy.

The Deacon:

Assist, preserve, pity, and keep us, O God, by Thy grace.

The Choir:

Lord, have mercy.

The Deacon:

Calling to mind the all holy, undefiled, most laudable and glorious Lady, the Mother of God, and Ever-Virgin Mary, with all the Saints, let us commend ourselves and each other, and our lives to Christ our God.

The Choir:

To Thee, O Lord.

The Priest (in a loud voice):

For unto Thee are due all glory, honour and

worship Father, Son and Holy Ghost, now and ever, world without end.

The Choir:

Amen.

The Deacon, having made a reverence, shall leave his place and shall stand before the Ikon of Christ, holding his Stole with three fingers of his right hand.

Then the Choir shall sing Psalm ciii. in antiphon:

Praise the Lord, O my Soul; and all that is within me praise His Holy Name.

Praise the Lord, O my soul: and forget not all His benefits;

Who forgiveth all thy sin: and healeth all thine infirmities;

Who saveth thy life from destruction: and crowneth thee with mercy and loving-kindness;

Who satisfieth thy mouth with good things: making thee young and lusty as an eagle.

The Lord executeth righteousness and judgment: for all them that are oppressed with wrong.

He shewed His ways unto Moses: His works unto the children of Israel.

The Lord is full of compassion and mercy: long-suffering, and of great goodness.

He will not be always chiding: neither keepeth He His anger for ever.

He hath not dealt with us after our sins: nor
rewarded us according to our wickednesses.

For look how high the heaven is in comparison of
the earth: so great is His mercy toward them that fear
Him.

Look how wide also the east is from the west: so
far hath he set our sins from us.

Yea, like as a father pitieth his own children:
even so is the Lord merciful unto them that fear Him.

For He knoweth whereof we are made: He
remembereth that we are but dust.

The days of man are but as grass: for he flourish-
eth as a flower of the field.

For as soon as the wind goeth over it, it is gone:
and the place thereof shall know it no more.

But the merciful goodness of the Lord endureth
for ever and ever upon them that fear Him: and His
righteousness upon children's children;

Even upon such as keep His covenant: and think
upon His Commandments to do them.

The Lord hath prepared His seat in Heaven: and
His Kingdom ruleth over all.

O praise the Lord, ye angels of His, ye that excel
in strength; ye that fulfil His commandment, and
hearken unto the voice of His words.

O praise the Lord, all ye His hosts: ye servants of
His that do His pleasure.

O speak good of the Lord, all ye works of His, in
all places of His dominion: praise thou the Lord, O
my soul.

Glory be to the Father, and to the Son: and to the Holy Ghost;

As it was in the beginning, is now and ever shall be: world without end. Amen.

Or on great Feasts its appointed substitute.

While the Choir sing, the Priest shall say privately the prayer of the First Antiphon as follows:

Lord our God whose power is boundless, whose glory is immeasurable, and whose compassion is infinite, and whose love for mankind is ineffable, look down, O Lord, in Thy tender mercy upon us, and upon this holy house. Vouchsafe to us, and to them that pray with us, the riches of Thy boundless goodness.

When the Antiphon has been sung, the Deacon shall return to his accustomed place, and shall say:

Again and yet again in peace, let us make our supplications to the Lord.

The Choir:

Lord, have mercy.

The Deacon:

Assist, preserve, pity, and keep us, O Lord, by Thy grace.

The Choir:

Lord, have mercy.

The Deacon:

Calling to mind the all-holy, undefiled, most laudable and glorious Lady, the Mother of God, and
Ever-Virgin Mary, with all the Saints, let us commend ourselves and each other and our lives to
Christ our God.

The Choir:

To Thee, O Lord.

*While the Deacon and Choir recite the above Litany, the
Priest shall say privately the prayer of the Second Antiphon:*

O Lord our God save Thy people and bless
Thine inheritance. Preserve the fulness of Thy
Church. Sanctify them that love the beauty of Thy
House. And in recompense glorify them with Thy
Divine power and forsake not them that put their
trust in Thee.

The Priest (in a loud voice).

For Thine is the majesty, the kingdom, the power
and the glory, the Father, the Son, and the Holy
Ghost now and ever world without end.

The Choir:

Amen.

The Deacon, having made a reverence, shall leave his place and shall stand before the Ikon of Christ, holding his Stole with three fingers of his right hand as before.

Then the Choir shall sing the Second Antiphon, Psalm cxlvi.

Praise the Lord, O my soul; whilst I live will I praise the Lord: yea, as long as I have any being, I will sing praises unto my God.

O put not your trust in princes, nor in any child of man: for there is no help in them.

For when the breath of man goeth forth he shall turn again to his earth: and then all his thoughts perish.

Blessed is he that hath the God of Jacob for his help: and whose hope is in the Lord his God;

Who made heaven and earth, the sea, and all that therein is: who keepeth his promise for ever;

Who helpeth them to right that suffer wrong: who feedeth the hungry.

The Lord looseth men out of prison: the Lord giveth sight to the blind.

The Lord helpeth them that are fallen: the Lord careth for the righteous.

The Lord careth for the strangers, he defendeth

the fatherless and widow: as for the way of the ungodly he turneth it upside down.

The Lord thy God, O Sion, shall be King for evermore: and throughout all generations.

Glory be to the Father, and to the Son, and to the Holy Ghost;

As it was in the beginning, is now and ever shall be: world without end.   Amen.

Or on great Feast Days its appointed substitute.

Then shall be sung the Anthem:

O Only Begotten Son and Word of God, Who art immortal, yet didst deign for our salvation to become incarnate of the Holy Mother of God, the Ever-Virgin Mary, and retaining Thy Divine Nature became man, Who wert crucified for us O Christ our God, and Who by death didst conquer Death, Who art of the Holy Trinity and art glorified together with the Father and the Holy Ghost.   Save us.

The Deacon:

Again and yet again in peace, let us make our supplications to the Lord.

The Choir:

Lord, have mercy.

The Deacon:

Assist, preserve, pity and keep us, O God, by Thy grace.

The Choir:

Lord, have mercy.

The Deacon:

Calling to mind the all-holy, undefiled, most laudable and glorious Lady, the Mother of God, and Ever-Virgin Mary, with all the Saints, let us commend ourselves and each other, and our lives to Christ our God.

The Choir:

To Thee, O Lord.

While the Deacon and Choir recite the above, the Priest shall say privately the prayer of the Third Antiphon:

O Thou Who hast given us grace at this time with one accord to make our common supplications unto Thee, and dost promise that when two or three are gathered together in Thy Name, Thou wilt grant their requests. Fulfil now, O Lord, the desires and petitions of Thy servants, as may be most expedient for them, granting them in this world knowledge of Thy truth, and in the world to come life everlasting.

The Priest:

For Thou art a just God, and loveth mankind, and unto Thee we ascribe glory with the Father, Son and the Holy Ghost, now and ever world without end.

The Choir.

Amen.

Then the Deacon shall enter the Sanctuary, while the Choir shall chant the Third Antiphon:

In Thy kingdom remember us: O Lord when Thou comest into Thy kingdom. Blessed are the poor in spirit, for theirs is the Kingdom of Heaven. Blessed are they that mourn, for they shall be comforted. Blessed are the meek, for they shall inherit the earth. Blessed are they who do hunger and thirst after righteousness, for they shall be filled. Blessed are the merciful, for they shall obtain mercy. Blessed are the pure in heart, for they shall see God. Blessed are the peacemakers, for they shall be called the children of God. Blessed are they which are persecuted for righteousness sake for theirs is the Kingdom of Heaven. Blessed are ye when men shall revile you, persecute you, say all manner of evil against you for My sake.

While the last portion of the Beatitudes is being sung, the Priest shall say in a low voice the Prayer of the Little Entrance:

O Master Lord our God, Who hast appointed in Heaven armies and hosts of Angels and Archangels for the ministry of Thy Glory; grant that with our entrance the Holy Angels may enter with us, and with us minister and glorify Thy goodness. For to Thee are due all glory, honour and worship, and to the Son and to the Holy Ghost now and ever, world without end. Amen.

Then the Priest shall take the Book of the Gospels from the Altar, and going then to the Deacon they shall both make the Lesser Entrance, preceded by the Reader bearing a lighted taper, and the Priest shall say:

Rejoice and be exceeding glad, for great is your reward in Heaven.

Then the Deacon, taking his stand before the Holy Door, shall say:

Master, Bless the Holy Entrance.

The Priest:

Blessed be the Entrance of Thy Saints, always now and ever world without end.

The Choir:

Amen.

Then the Deacon shall go to the Priest, who shall kiss the Book of the Gospels, and the Deacon shall stand before the centre of the Holy Door, and elevate the Gospels, saying in a loud voice:

In wisdom arise.

Then both shall go to the Altar, and the Deacon shall lay the Gospels thereon, whilst the Choir sing:

O come let us worship and fall down before the Lord. Save us, O Son of God, seated amongst the Saints who sing unto Thee. Alleluia.[1]

Then shall be sung the Hymn and the Collect proper for the day.

Then the Priest shall say privately the Prayer of the Trisagion ("The Thrice Holy"):

O Holy God, Who dost rest in the Holies, Who art extolled in the Trisagion by the Seraphim, and glorified by the Cherubim, and adored by all the Heavenly Powers, Thou Who out of nothingness didst call all things into life, Who didst create man

[1] On Sundays the words " Who didst rise again from the dead " are substituted ; and on Feasts the refrain from the Antiphon proper to the day.

after Thine own image and likeness, and didst adorn him with Thy Heavenly grace, Thou Who givest to him that asketh, wisdom and understanding, Who despisest not a sinner, but through repentance dost offer a sure path unto salvation, Thou who hast vouchsafed that we, Thy humble and unworthy servants, should now stand before the glory of Thy Holy Altar, render unto Thee the adoration and praise which are Thy due; receive Lord from the mouths of us sinners the Hymn of Trisagion; and visit us in Thine abundant mercy. Forgive us our sins, voluntary and involuntary; sanctify our souls and our bodies; and grant that we may serve Thee in holiness all the days of our life, through the intercession of the Holy Mother of God, and of all the Saints who have been pleasing unto Thee from the beginning.

And while the Choir are singing the last Hymn the Deacon, holding the Stole with three fingers, shall say to the Priest, as both bow their heads:

Master, Bless the moment of the Trisagion.

The Priest shall bless the Deacons with the sign of the Cross, and say aloud:

Holy art Thou, O our God, and unto Thee we ascribe glory, to the Father, to the Son, and to the Holy Ghost, now and ever.

*And when the Hymn is finished the Deacon shall approach
the Holy Door, and, pointing to the Ikon of Christ, shall
say:*

O Lord, save those who fear Thee, and hear us.

*Then he shall point in like manner to the congregation, and
say:*

World without end.

The Choir:

Amen.

Holy God, Holy and Mighty, Holy and Immortal,
have mercy upon us *(five times)*.[1]

The Deacon shall then say to the Priest:

Master, give the order.

*And they shall approach the Holy Throne, and the Priest
as he goeth shall say:*

Blessed is he that cometh in the name of the Lord.

The Deacon:

Master, bless the throne.

At Christmas, at the Epiphany, on the eve of Palm Sunday, on
Holy Saturdays, during Eastertide and at Pentecost instead of the Trisagion they shall sing " As many as have been baptised into Christ have
put on Christ.   Alleluia."

E

The Priest:

Blessed are Thou on the Throne of Thy Glory, Who sitteth upon the Cherubim always now and ever world without end.

The Priest shall then take his seat beside the High Place looking toward the south.

And when the Choir have finished singing the Trisagion the Deacon shall say:

Let us attend.

The Priest:

Peace be with you all.

The Reader:

And with Thy Spirit.

The Deacon:

Wisdom.

The Reader shall say the Prokimenon: [1]

The Reader:

The lesson from the Epistle of the Holy Apostle (N. to N.).

[1] The Prokimenon or Gradual is a short anthem sung before the Epistle. It consists of a verse and response generally taken from the Psalms.

The Deacon:

Let us attend.

The Reader then readeth the Epistle. While the Epistle is being read the Deacon shall take the Censer, and approaching the Priest receive his blessing; and cense the Altar, the Sanctuary, the Priest, and people; and when the Epistle is finished the Priest shall say:

Peace be upon Thee.

The Reader:

And with Thy Spirit.

The Deacon:

Wisdom.

The Reader:

Alleluia.

The Priest then says privately the Prayer of the Gospel as follows:

O Lord and lover of men; illumine our hearts with the pure light of Thy Divine knowledge, and open the eyes of our understanding that we may comprehend the precepts of Thy Gospel. Implant in us likewise the fear of Thy blessed commandments, that we, trampling upon all fleshly lusts, may attain the joy of Heavenly Life, both thinking and doing such things as shall well please Thee. For Thou art the Light of our souls and of our bodies, O Christ our God. And unto Thee do we ascribe glory, together with the Father who is from everlasting, and the Holy Blessed and vivifying Spirit, now and ever world without end. Amen.

Then the Deacon, drawing near to the Priest, shall lay aside the Censer, and bowing to him, and holding with the tips of his fingers his Stole and the Book of the Gospels in the place of the Altar whereon it lies, shall say:

Master, bless him who proclaimeth the Holy Apostle Evangelist N.

And the Priest, signing him with the sign of the Cross, shall say:

May God through the intercession of the Holy glorious Apostle and Evangelist N. grant utterance and power unto thee who announceth the Word to the fulfilment of the Gospel of His Blessed Son our Lord Jesus Christ.

The Deacon:

Amen.

*And having done reverence to the Gospel, he taketh it and
going through the Holy Door, preceded by a taper, shall
stand upon the Tribune or in the place prepared, and the
Priest, standing before the Altar, looking toward the
West, shall say in a loud voice:*

Wisdom.   Stand ye up.   Let us hear the Holy
Gospel.   Peace be with ye all.

The Choir:

And with Thy Spirit.

The Deacon:

The lesson from the Holy Gospel according to *N.*

The Choir:

Glory to Thee, O God.   Glory to Thee.

The Priest:

Let us attend.

*And the Deacon readeth the Gospel, and when he hath
finished the Priest shall say to the Deacon:*

Peace be unto thee, who hast announced the good
tidings.

*Then the Deacon, standing in his accustomed place, shall
say.*

Let us say with all our soul, with all our mind,

The Choir:

Lord, have mercy.

The Deacon:

O Lord Almighty God of our fathers, we beseech Thee hearken and have mercy.

The Choir:

Lord, have mercy.

The Deacon:

Have mercy upon us, O God, according to Thy great mercy.   We beseech Thee hearken and have mercy upon us.

The Choir:

Lord, have mercy *(thrice)*.

The Deacon:

For our Holy Synod N.; for our Archbishop N.; for the venerable Presbytery, for the Diaconate in Christ, for all the clergy, and the laity.

The Choir:

Lord, have mercy *(thrice)*.

The Deacon:

For our God-fearing army and navy.

The Choir:

Lord, have mercy *(thrice)*.

The Deacon:

For our brethren, the Priests, for all Monks, and for our Brotherhood in Christ.

The Choir:

Lord, have mercy *(thrice)*.

The Deacon:

For the blessed and ever memorable Holy orthodox Patriarchs, the God-fearing Czars and Czaritzas, and for the founders of this Holy Temple. For all our Fathers and Brethren who have fallen asleep before us, and lie here; and for all the orthodox in whatever part of the earth they may rest.

The Choir:

Lord, have mercy *(thrice)*.

The Deacon:

We pray for those who bring forth the fruit of good deeds in this Holy and Venerable Temple; for those who labour in its service; for the singers, and for the congregation here present who wait expectantly Thy great and abundant mercy.

The Choir:

Lord, have mercy *(thrice)*.

The Priest:

For Thou art a merciful God and lovest mankind, and to Thee we ascribe glory and to the Son and to the Holy Ghost, now and ever world without end.

The Choir:

Amen.

The Deacon:

Let us pray to the Lord.

The Choir:

Lord, have mercy.

The Priest:

O Lord, our Almighty and Almerciful God in due humility we make our common supplication unto Thee. Beneath the shelter of Thy loving-kindness preserve from all evil our God-fearing Emperor N. Let Thy Holy Angels watch over him, and suffer not

his enemies to prevail against him; nor any son of
iniquity to be a cause of offence unto him.   Grant
unto him length of days, and an abundance of
strength, and enable him to act in all things for Thy
Glory and for the welfare of his people; so that we
rejoicing in Thine abundant grace toward him, every
day and every hour, may bless and exalt Thy Holy
Name, O Father, Son, and Holy Ghost, now and ever
world without end.

The Choir:

Amen.

*And if there be any offerings on behalf of the dead the
Deacon shall say:*

Have mercy upon us, O God, according to the
greatness of Thy mercy, we beseech Thee; hearken
and have mercy.

The Choir:

Lord, have mercy *(thrice)*.

The Deacon:

Furthermore we pray for the repose of the
servants of God N. N. who have departed this life,
and that Thou wilt pardon all their sins, voluntary
and involuntary.

The Choir:

Lord, have mercy.

The Deacon:

That the Lord God will number their souls among those of the just.

The Choir:

Lord, have mercy.

The Deacon:

The Grace of God, the Kingdom of Heaven, and the remission of our sins. Grant us O Christ our King, Ever-living and our God.

The Choir:

Hear us, O Lord.

The Deacon:

Let us pray to the Lord.

The Choir:

Lord, have mercy.

The Priest shall say privately:

O God of Heaven and of all flesh, Who hast over-

come death, and overthrown the Devil, and given life
to the world; give rest to the souls of Thy departed
servants N. N. in a place of joy, a verdant garden of
repose, where sickness and sorrow be no more.
Pardon all their transgressions, voluntary and
involuntary, in word or deed or thought. For Thou
art a just God and lovest mankind; and no man liveth
that is without sin. For Thou only art perfect, and
Thy goodness endureth for ever; and Thy word is
truth. *(Aloud)* For Thou art the Resurrection and
the Life and the Refuge of Thy departed servants
N. N. O Christ our God: And unto Thee do we ascribe
glory, together with the Father Who is from everlasting; and to the Holy Ghost the Giver of Life, now and
ever world without end.

The Choir:

Amen.

The Deacon:

Pray ye unto the Lord O ye Catechumens.

The Choir:

Lord, have mercy.

The Deacon:

Ye faithful, pray unto the Lord for the
Catechumens that He may have mercy upon them.

The Choir:

Lord, have mercy.

The Deacon:

That He may reveal to them the Gospel of Truth.

The Choir:

Lord, have mercy.

The Deacon:

That He may unite them to His Holy Catholic and Apostolic Church.

The Choir:

Lord, have mercy.

The Deacon:

Preserve them. Have mercy upon them. Sustain them, and continually guard them, O God.

The Choir:

Lord, have mercy.

The Deacon:

Bow your heads unto the Lord, ye Catechumens.

The Choir:

To Thee, O Lord.

Then shall the Priest say the Prayer of the Catechumens in a low voice:

O Lord our God, Who dwellest on high and beholdest the humble; Who didst send forth for the salvation of mankind Thine Only Begotten Son, our Lord Jesus Christ. Look down upon Thy servants, the Catechumens, who have bowed their heads to Thee. Grant unto them in due season, through the cleansing waters of regeneration, the forgiveness of sins, and the robe of immortality. Unite them to Thy Holy Catholic and Apostolic Church; and include them amongst the number of Thine elect. *(Aloud)* That they also together with us may glorify Thine honourable and majestic Name Father, Son and Holy Ghost, now and ever world without end.

The Choir:

Amen.

The Priest shall then unfold the Corporal and make the sign of the Cross thereon with the Sponge, which he then kisseth and layeth aside.

The Deacon:

Let all the Catechumens depart. Depart, all ye

Catechumens, depart. Let all the Catechumens depart. Let no Catechumen remain. But let us who are in the Faith again make our supplications unto the Lord.

The Choir:

Lord, have mercy.

Then shall the Catechumens depart.

III. THE LITURGY OF THE FAITHFUL

The Priest says privately the first Prayer of the Faithful:

We give thanks unto Thee, Lord God of Sabaoth, Who hast vouchsafed unto us to stand now before Thine Altar, and to fall down in adoration for Thy long suffering mercy towards our sins and the errors of Thy people.   Accept, O Lord, our supplications. Make us worthy to offer to Thee our prayers and supplications, and the unbloody sacrifice for Thy people.   Strengthen us whom Thou hast placed in Thy Ministry with the grace of the Holy Ghost that we may blamelessly and without offence in the pure testimony of our conscience call upon Thee at all times and in all places.   Hear us and be merciful unto us in the abundance of Thy goodness.

[*Or if the Liturgy of St. Basil be used:*

Thou, O Lord, Who hast disclosed to us the great mystery of salvation, and hast graciously permitted us Thy humble and unworthy servants to be the ministers of Thy Holy Altar.   Render us by the power of the Holy Ghost worthy of this divine office, that standing uncondemned before Thy Holy glory, we may offer to Thee our oblation of praise. For Thou art He that workest all things in all men. Grant, O Lord, that our sacrifice may be acceptable and well pleasing in Thy sight, in mitigation of our offences, and of the errors of Thy people.]

The Deacon:

Assist, preserve, pity and have mercy upon us, and keep us, O God, by Thy grace.

The Choir:

Lord, have mercy.

The Priest:

For unto Thee are due all honour, glory, and adoration, Father, Son, and Holy Ghost now and ever world without end.

The Choir:

Amen.

The Deacon:

Again and yet again let us pray to the Lord in peace.

The Choir:

Lord, have mercy.

The Deacon:

For the peace that is from Above, and for the salvation of our souls, let us pray to the Lord.

The Choir:

Lord, have mercy.

Then shall the Priest say privately the Second Prayer of the Faithful:

Again and oftimes we fall down before Thee and beseech Thee, O Gracious God, lover of mankind, to hearken to our prayers, and to purify our souls and bodies from all defilement of the flesh and of the spirit. And grant that we may stand before Thy Holy Altar blameless and uncondemned. Grant, O God, to those who make their supplications life, spiritual wisdom, and understanding. Grant that they may at all times serve Thee blamelessly in fear and love; and that they may in innocence partake of Thy Holy Mysteries, and be deemed worthy of everlasting life.

[Or if the Liturgy of St. Basil the Great be used:

O God, Who in Thy mercy and bounty has visited our lowliness: Who hast appointed us Thy humble and unworthy servants to serve the Holy glory of Thine Altar. Strengthen us by the power of the Holy Ghost for this Divine office; and grant that as we

F

open our lips we may worthily invoke the grace of
Thy Holy Spirit, upon the oblation we are about to
offer.]

The Deacon:

Wisdom.

*Then shall the Deacon enter the Sanctuary through the
North Door.*

The Priest:

That being ever guarded by Thy Might we may
ascribe glory to Thee, Father, Son and Holy Ghost,
now and ever world without end.

The Choir:

Amen.

The Choir shall then sing the Hymn of the Cherubim:

Let us who mystically represent the Cherubim
sing a Holy hymn to the quickening Trinity. *(Here
the Great Entrance with the Holy Gifts is made).* Lay
aside at this time all worldly cares that we may
receive the King of Glory and His invisible company
of Heavenly Hosts. Alleluia, Alleluia, Alleluia.

*While the Choir sing the Hymn the Priest shall say
privately:*

None among them that are bound by fleshy

desires, and sensual pleasures is worthy to approach
Thee, to serve Thee, or to sacrifice unto Thee, O King
of Glory. For Thy Ministry is a task fearful even to
the Heavenly Hosts. Yet through Thine ineffable
and boundless love Thou unchanging didst become
man, and assume the title of our High Priest, and
didst commit to us the ministry of this bloodless
sacrifice O God of all. Thou alone, O our God, rulest
over things visible and invisible, and sittest upon the
throne of the Cherubim, Thou Lord of the Seraphim
and King of Israel. Who alone art Holy and dwellest
amongst the Saints. Thee I importune Who alone
art good and hearest us. Hearken unto me a sinner
and Thine unworthy servant, and cleanse my soul
and my heart from iniquities. Fortify me who have
been endued with the grace of the Priesthood, with
the might of Thy Holy Spirit, that I may stand by this
Thy Holy Altar, and sacrifice Thine immaculate Body
and Thy precious Blood. Bowing my head I
approach Thee, and implore Thee neither to turn Thy
Face away from me, nor to cast me out from the
number of Thy Sons. Graciously grant that these
gifts be offered to Thee by me a sinner, Thine
unworthy servant. Thou that offerest and art offered,
receivest and art received, O Christ our God to Thee
and to the Father Who is from everlasting and to the
Holy Ghost the quickener do we ascribe glory and
honour, now and ever world without end.

Then the Deacon shall take the Censer, and having received the Priest's blessing shall cense the Holy Altar and the Sanctuary, saying privately:

Have mercy upon me, O God, after Thy great goodness: according to the multitude of Thy mercies do away mine offences.

Wash me throughly from my wickedness: and cleanse me from my sin.

For I acknowledge my faults: and my sin is ever before me.

Against Thee only have I sinned, and done this evil in Thy sight: that Thou mightest be justified in Thy saying, and clear when thou art judged.

Behold I was shapen in wickedness: and in sin hath my mother conceived me.

But lo, thou requirest truth in the inward parts: and shalt make me to understand wisdom secretly.

Thou shalt purge me with hyssop, and I shall be clean: Thou shalt wash me and I shall be whiter than snow.

Thou shalt make me hear of joy and gladness: that the bones which Thou hast broken may rejoice.

Turn Thy face from my sins: and put out all my misdeeds.

Make me a clean heart, O God: and renew a right spirit within me.

Cast me not away from Thy presence: and take not Thy Holy Spirit from me.

O give me the comfort of Thy help again : and establish me with Thy free Spirit.

Then shall I teach Thy ways unto the wicked : and sinners shall be converted unto Thee.

Deliver me from blood-guiltiness, O God, Thou that art the God of my health : and my tongue shall sing of Thy righteousness.

Thou shalt open my lips, O Lord : and my mouth shall show Thy praise.

For Thou desirest no sacrifice, else would I give it Thee : but Thou delightest not in burnt-offerings.

The sacrifices of God is a troubled spirit : a broken and contrite heart, O God, shalt thou not despise.

O be favourable and gracious unto Sion : build Thou the walls of Jerusalem.

Then shalt thou be pleased with the sacrifice of righteousness, with the burnt-offerings and oblations : then shall they offer young bullocks upon Thy Altar.

Then the Priest and the Deacon shall stand before the Altar, and thrice making reverence, shall say:

O God, be merciful to me a sinner.

Then the Deacon shall say to the Priest:

Master, raise it.

And the Priest, taking the Veil and placing it on the left shoulder of the Deacon, shall say:

Lift up your hands in the Sanctuary and bless the Lord.

Then taking the Paten he shall place it reverently upon the head of the Deacon, who still holdeth the Censer. And the Priest shall take in his hand the Chalice, and they shall go forth through the North Door, preceded by a Taper; and, both facing the people, the Deacon shall say:

May the Lord God remember in His Kingdom our most God-fearing Sovereign and Emperor N. of all the Russias now and ever world without end.

The Priest:

And may the Lord God remember in His Kingdom all the reigning house, now and ever, world without end.

The Deacon:

May the Lord God remember in His Kingdom the Holy Synod of Russia and our Archbishop N., now and ever, world without end.

The Priest:

May the Lord God remember in His Kingdom all orthodox Christians, now and ever, world without end.

The Choir:

Amen.

And the Deacon, going within the Holy Doors, shall stand on the right hand, and when the Priest is about to enter in shall say to him:

May the Lord God remember thy Priesthood in His Kingdom.

The Priest:

May the Lord God remember Thy Diaconate in His Kingdom now and ever world without end.

Then the Priest shall set the Chalice upon the Altar to the right, and taking the Paten from the head of the Deacon he shall place it to the left of the Altar, saying:

The noble Joseph took Thine Immaculate Body from the Cross, and wrapped it in fine linen with spices, and laid it in a new sepulchre with fitting ceremony: As God Thy Body was in the grave, and Thy Soul was in Hell. Thou wert in Paradise with the thief, and Thou wert on the Throne with the Father, and the Holy Ghost O Christ Who art Infinite, and in all verily Thy tomb giveth life, and is more beautiful than Paradise; more splendid than any Royal chamber, O Christ Fountain of our Resurrection.

Then shall he take the Veils from the Paten and from the Chalice, and laying them on one side of the Altar shall take the Veil from the Deacon's shoulder, and having censed it shall cover therewith the Holy Gifts, and say:

The noble Joseph took Thine Immaculate Body from the Cross and wrapped it in fine linen with spices, and laid it in a new sepulchre with fitting ceremony.

Then he shall take the Censer from the hands of the Deacon and thrice cense the Holy Gifts, saying:

O Lord exalt Thou Sion in Thy sight, and build Thou the walls of Jerusalem. Thou shalt be pleased with the sacrifice of righteousness, with oblations, and burnt offerings, and young bullocks shall be offered upon Thine Altar.

Then he shall give the Censer to the Deacon and bow his head, saying:

Remember me, O brother and fellow minister.

And the Deacon shall say to him:

May the Lord God remember thy Priesthood in His Kingdom.

The Deacon, also bowing his head and holding his Stole with three fingers of his right hand, shall say to the Priest:

Pray for me Holy master.

The Priest:

May the Holy Ghost come upon thee, and the power of the Most High overshadow thee.

The Deacon:

May that Spirit be fellow minister with us all the days of our life.

Remember me, Holy master.

The Priest:

May the Lord God remember thee in His Kingdom always, now and ever world without end.

The Deacon:

Let us accomplish our supplications unto the Lord.

The Choir:

Lord have mercy.

The Deacon:

For the precious gifts now spread forth let us make our supplications to the Lord.

The Choir:

Lord, have mercy.

The Deacon:

For this Holy House, and for them that with faith, reverence, and in the fear of God, have entered it, let us make our supplications to the Lord.

The Choir:

Lord, have mercy.

The Deacon:

That we may be delivered from all afflictions, passions, dangers, and necessities, let us make our supplications to the Lord.

The Choir:

Lord, have mercy.

The Deacon:

Assist, preserve, pity, and keep us, O God, by Thy Grace.

The Choir:

Lord, have mercy.

The Deacon:

That the whole day may be perfect, peaceful, and without sin, let us make our supplications to the Lord.

The Choir:

Grant this, O Lord.

The Deacon:

That an Angel of Peace may be the faithful guide and guardian of our souls, let us make our supplications to the Lord.

The Choir:

Grant this, O Lord.

The Deacon:

For the pardon and remission of our sins and transgressions, let us make our supplications to the Lord.

The Choir:

Grant this, O Lord.

The Deacon:

For all things that are profitable both to our souls and bodies, and for the peace of the world, let us make our supplications to the Lord.

The Choir:

Grant this, O Lord.

The Deacon:

That we may pass the remainder of our life in peace and penitence, let us make our supplications to the Lord.

The Choir:

Grant this, O Lord.

The Deacon:

For a Christian termination to our life, painless and without shame, and full of peace, and for a good defence before the dread Tribunal of Christ, let us make our supplications to the Lord.

The Choir:

Grant this. O Lord.

The Deacon:

Calling to mind the most Holy, Undefiled, most laudable, and glorious Lady, the Mother of God, and Ever-Virgin Mary, with all the Saints, let us commend ourselves and each other and our lives to Christ our God.

The Choir:

To Thee, O Lord.

While this Ektene is being recited, the Priest shall say privately the Prayer of Oblation:

O Lord God, Who alone art Holy, Who accepteth the sacrifice of praise from them that call upon Thee with their whole hearts. Receive also the supplication of us sinners, and grant that it may reach Thy Holy Altar, and enable us to present gifts to Thee, and spiritual sacrifices of our sins, and for the errors of Thy people. And mercifully grant that we may obtain grace in Thy sight, that this our offering may be acceptable unto Thee, and that the excellent spirit of Thy grace may dwell within us, and upon these gifts now presented to Thee and upon all Thy people.

The Priest (in a loud voice):

Through the bounty of Thine Only Begotten Son, with Whom thou art glorified together with the most Holy and Good and quickening Spirit now and ever world without end.

The Choir:

Amen.

The Priest:

Peace be with you.

The Choir:

And with Thy Spirit.

The Deacon:

Let us love one another, that we may with one mind confess.

The Choir:

Father, Son, and Holy Ghost, the consubstantial and undivided Trinity.

The Deacon:

The doors. The doors. Let us attend in wisdom.

The Choir:

I believe in one God, the Father Almighty, Maker of Heaven and Earth, and of all things visible and invisible, and in one Lord Jesus Christ the Only Begotten Son of God, Begotten of His Father before all the worlds; Light of Light, Very God of Very God, Begotten not made; being of one Essence with the Father; by whom all things were made; Who, for us, men, and for our salvation, came down from Heaven, and was incarnate by the Holy Ghost of the Virgin Mary, and was made man. And was crucified also for us under Pontius Pilate, and suffered and was buried. And the third day He rose again, according to the Scriptures. And ascended into Heaven, and sitteth on the right hand of the Father. And He shall come again with glory to judge both the quick and the dead; Whose kingdom shall have no end.

And I believe in the Holy Ghost, the Lord and Giver of Life, Who proceedeth from the Father, Who with the Father and the Son together is worshipped and glorified. Who spake by the Prophets. In one Holy Catholic and Apostolic Church. I acknowledge one Baptism for the remission of sins. I look for the Resurrection of the dead, and the Life of the world to come. Amen.

The Deacon:

Let us stand with reverence, fear and attention that we may offer the Holy Oblation in peace.

The Choir:

The grace of peace, the sacrifice of praise.

The Priest shall bow before the Altar and say privately:

I will love Thee, O Lord, my strength. The Lord is my strong rock and my deliverer *(thrice).*

And he shall kiss first the cover of the Paten, and the top of the Chalice, and the edge of the Altar, and if there be several Priests they shall all kiss the Holy Vessels and each other on the shoulder. Then the Priest shall say:

Christ is in our midst.

And the Deacon shall answer:

He is and shall be.

The Priest shall then fan the Holy Elements, and taking the Veil lay it on one side, saying:

The Grace of our Lord Jesus Christ, and the love of God, the Father, and the Fellowship of the Holy Ghost be with you all.

The Choir:

And with Thy Spirit.

The Priest, pointing upward:

Let us lift up our hearts.

The Choir:

We lift them up unto the Lord.

The Priest:

Let us give thanks unto the Lord.

The Choir:

It is meet and right to worship the Father, the Son, and the Holy Ghost the consubstantial, and undivided Trinity.

The Priest, bowing, shall say privately:

It is meet and right to praise Thee, to bless Thee, and to give thanks unto Thee, to worship Thee, in every place of Thy Dominion. For Thou art God, ineffable, inconceivable, invisible, incomprehensible, from everlasting to everlasting, and such are Thine only Begotten Son, and the Holy Ghost. Thou broughtest us from nothing into being, and when we were fallen didst raise us up again, and didst seek by all means to bring us to Heaven, and to give us an inheritance in Thy Kingdom. For these and all other Thy mercies, whether known to us or unknown, manifest or concealed, we give thanks to Thee and to Thine Only Begotten Son and to the Holy Ghost. For this ministry which Thou hast deigned to receive at our hands, we give thanks unto Thee, seeing Thou art encompassed by thousands of Archangels and tens of thousands of Angels, by the Cherubim and Seraphim six-winged and many-eyed, who aloft borne on their pinions sing, proclaim, and cry aloud that hymn of triumph.

[Or if the Liturgy of St. Basil be used, this Prayer said by the Priest in a low voice, bowing down before the Altar:

O Sovereign Lord, God the Father, who art Almighty and adorable; it is indeed very meet, right and our bounden duty that we should sing praises to Thee. We bless Thee, we worship Thee, we give thanks to Thee, we glorify Thee the only true God; and with contrite heart and humble spirit we offer to Thee this our reasonable service. For it is Thou Who hast called us to the knowledge of Thy truth.

G

But who can worthily proclaim Thy power, shew forth Thy praise, and tell of all Thy wondrous works? O Lord of all things, of Heaven, and of earth, and of all created things both visible and invisible, who sittest upon the throne of glory, and beholdest the vast abyss. Thou Who art from all time invisible, inscrutable, incomprehensible, and unchangeable; Father of our Lord Jesus Christ, the great God and Saviour of our hope, who is the express image of Thy goodness, who shows forth Thee His Father, who is the living Lord God before all ages, Wisdom, Life, Holiness, Power, the true Light through Whom was manifested the Holy Spirit, the Spirit of Truth, the Grace of Adoption, and Pledge of our Future Inheritance, the First Fruits of eternal good things, the life-giving Power, and the Fountain of Holiness; by Whose power all reasonable and intelligent creatures do serve and praise Thee. For all things do serve Thee, Angels, Archangels, Thrones, Dominions, Principalities, Authorities, Powers, the many-eyed Cherubim and Seraphim with six wings who with twain do cover their faces, and with twain their feet, and with twain do fly crying one to another continually with never ceasing praise.]

The Choir:

Holy, Holy, Holy, Lord God of Sabaoth, Heaven and Earth are full of the Majesty of Thy

glory. Hosannah in the highest: Blessed is he that
cometh in the Name of the Lord, Hosannah in the
highest.

*Then the Deacon shall take the Asterisk from the Paten,
and signing it with the sign of the Cross, shall kiss it and
lay it upon one side. He shall then go and stand on the
right side of the Altar, and the Priest shall say in a low
voice:*

We also with these blessed powers, O Lord Thou
Lover of mankind, cry out and say Holy art Thou and
most Holy, Thou and Thine Only Begotten Son, and
Thy Holy Spirit. Holy and most Holy art Thou, and
great is Thy Glory Who didst so love the world that
Thou gavest Thine Only Begotten Son, that whoso
believeth in Him should not perish, but have everlasting life. He came into the world and fulfilled
all that which was appointed for Him to do for our
sakes. In the same night whereon He was delivered
up, nay rather in which He delivered up Himself to
suffer death for the Life of the world; He took bread
in His Holy, Immaculate, and Undefiled Hands, and
when He had given thanks, He blessed it, sanctified
it, broke it, and gave it to His Disciples and Apostles
saying,

*[Or if the Liturgy of St. Basil be used, the following
Prayer is substituted:*

With those blessed powers, O Merciful Lord, we

unworthy sinners do also cry aloud and say Holy art
Thou in truth, Thy Holiness is perfect, and infinite,
manifesting itself in all Thy works, for in righteousness and true judgment hast Thou ordained all
things. When Thou didst form man out of the dust
of the earth and honoured him, O God, with Thine
Own Image, didst place him in a Paradise of
pleasure, promising him life eternal and eternal
happiness, as reward for obeying Thy commandments. But when overcome by the subtleties of the
Serpent, he transgressed Thy Word, and through his
sinfulness became subject to death, Thou, O God, in
Thy just judgment, didst drive him out of Paradise,
and reduce him to earth whence he was taken, but
didst prepare for him a new birth to everlasting life
which is in Thy Christ. For Thou wast not always
wrath with Thy creatures, or for ever unmindful of
the work of Thine Own Hands, but in Thy abundant
pity, didst in divers ways visit him with Thy saving
care. Thou didst send Thy prophets, didst show
mighty works through Thy saints who pleased Thee
in all ages. Thou spakest to us by the mouth of Thy
servants the prophets who foretold to us the salvation
that was to come. Thou didst appoint the law for
our discretion, and guardian angels for our guidance.
And when the fulness of time was come Thou didst
speak unto us by Thy Son by Whom Thou hadst
made the world. Who being the brightness of Thy
Glory, and the true image of Thy Person, upholding
all things by the word of His power, deemed it no

robbery to be equal to Thee His God and His Father. Although He was God from all eternity, descended from Heaven and held converse with mankind, was incarnate of the Virgin Mary, didst assume the form of humility, making Himself in His abasement like unto us, that He might raise us to the image of His glory. For as by man sin entered into the world, and by sin death, so it seemed good to Thine Only Begotten Son Who is in the bosom of Thee, His God and Father, being born of a woman, the Holy Mother of God and Ever Virgin Mary, and ordained to triumph over sin in His own flesh that those who died in Adam might live again in Him Thy Christ. And dwelling as a citizen in this world, instructing us in the way of salvation, He brought us from our idolatry to the knowledge of Thee our true God and Father, purchasing us to Himself for a peculiar people, a royal priesthood and Holy nation, and having baptised us with water for the remission of our sin, and sanctified us with the Holy Ghost, gave Himself as ransom to redeem us from death, to which we were held in bondage by our sins. And passing by the Cross into Hell that he might fulfil all things in Himself, He loosed the pains of Death; and rising again the third day, did prepare a way for the resurrection of all flesh from the dead, and forasmuch as it was impossible that the Prince of Life should be held of corruption. He became the first fruits of them that slept, and the first born from the dead that He might be the First of all in all things. And ascending into

Heaven, He sat down at the right hand of Thy Majesty on high, whence He shall come again to render to every man according to his works. And as a memorial of His saving Passion, He has left to us these gifts which we have now offered according to His command. For when He was about to go forth to His voluntary, glorious, and life-giving Death, in the same night wherein He gave up Himself for the Life of the World, taking bread into His Holy and Immaculate Hands, and presenting it to Thee His God and His Father, He gave thanks, blessed, hallowed, and brake it. He gave it to His Holy disciples and apostles, saying:—]

The Priest then bows his head, and devoutly holding up his right hand, blesseth the Holy Bread, saying in a loud voice:

Take, eat, this is my Body which is broken for you for the remission of sins.

As the Priest says this, the Deacon shall point out to him the Paten, holding his Stole with three fingers of his right hand.

The Choir:
Amen.

The Priest:
And in like manner after supper He took the Cup, saying,

As the Priest says this the Deacon pointeth to the Chalice.

[Or if the Liturgy of St. Basil the Great be used the Priest says secretly:

In a like manner giving thanks and taking, mixing, blessing, and sanctifying the Cup of the fruit of the vine.

The Priest, holding up his right hand and blessing it, says in a loud voice:

He gave it to His Holy disciples and apostles, saying,]

Drink ye all of this.   This is my Blood of the New Testament which is shed for you and for many for the remission of sins.

The Choir:

Amen.

The Priest (in a low voice):

In remembrance therefore of this command of our Saviour, and of all those things which He did for us; of His Cross, His Burial, His Resurrection on the third day, and His Ascension into Heaven, His sitting down at Thy right Hand, and of His second and glorious advent.

[If the Liturgy of St. Basil the Great be used:

Do this in remembrance of Me; for as oft as ye eat of this Bread, and drink of this Cup, ye shew forth My Death and confess My Resurrection. Wherefore we also, O Lord, bear in remembrance those things which He suffered for our redemption, His life-giving Cross, His burial of three days, His resurrection from the dead, and His Ascension into Heaven, and His sitting at the right Hand of Thee His God and Father, and of His glorious and terrible second coming.

The Priest (in a loud voice):

Thine own, out of Thine own, we offer unto Thee through all and for all.]

Then the Deacon, crossing his hands, lifts up the Paten and the Chalice, and making with them the sign of the Cross, shall bow reverently.

The Choir:

We praise Thee, we bless Thee, we give thanks unto Thee, O Lord, and make our supplications unto Thee, O Lord our God.

Then the Priest, bowing, shall say privately:

We offer to Thee this reasonable and bloodless sacrifice, and beg, pray, and beseech Thee to send down Thine Holy Spirit upon us and upon these gifts spread before Thee.

[Or if the Liturgy of St. Basil the Great be used the following:

Wherefore, O most Holy Lord, do we sinners, Thy unworthy servants who have been counted worthy to minister unto Thee, not on account of our own righteousness, for indeed we have done no good thing, but according to Thy mercy and compassion, which Thou hast liberally bestowed upon us, approach this Holy Altar; and laying before Thee these symbols[1] of the Holy Body and Blood of Thy Christ, we beseech Thee and invoke Thee, O Thou Holy of Holies, of Thy gracious goodness, to send down Thy Holy Spirit upon us and upon these gifts, and to bless, to sanctify, and to perfect them.]

The Deacon shall then lay aside the Veil, and approaching the Priest shall with him bow down thrice before the Altar, both praying privately as follows:

God be merciful to me a sinner. *(Thrice)*

O Lord Who didst send Thy Holy Spirit to Thine Apostles at the third hour. Take Him not from us, O merciful God, but renew Him in us who make our supplications unto Thee. *(And)*

---

[1] This word is used in the same sense in St. Macarius, St. Gregory Naz., St. Theodoret, St. John Damascene, St. Mark of Ephesus, and others, and appears to refer to the elements only before consecration.

Create in me a clean heart, O God, and renew a right spirit within me. Cast me not away from Thy presence. *(And)*

Glory be to the Father, and to the Son, and to the Holy Ghost.

Blessed art Thou Christ our God who didst fill the fishermen with wisdom, enduing them with Thy Holy Spirit, and by them didst bring the whole world into Thy net, O lover of mankind. Glory be to Thee.

When the Highest came down and confounded the tongues, He divided the peoples; but when He sent down the tongues of fire He united mankind, and we praise with one voice the Holy Ghost.

Then the Deacon, bowing his head, shall point with his Stole to the Holy Bread, and say in a low voice:

Bless, Master, the Holy Bread.

And the Priest shall stand up, and thrice making the sign of the Cross on the Holy Gifts, says in a low voice:

Make this Bread the precious Body Thy Christ.

The Deacon:

Amen.

[Or if the Liturgy of St. Basil the Great be used:

Make this bread in very truth the precious Body of our Lord and God, our Saviour Jesus Christ.]

The Deacon again:

Bless, Master, the Holy Cup.

The Priest, blessing it, says:

And that which is in this Cup, the precious Blood of Thy Christ.

The Deacon:

Amen.

The Deacon shall then point with his Stole to both the Holy Things, and say:

Master, give the blessing.

And the Priest, blessing both with his hands:

Changing them by Thy Holy Spirit.

The Deacon:

Amen.   *(Thrice.)*

The Priest and Deacon here prostrate themselves.

Then bowing to the Priest, he shall say:

Master, remember me a sinner.

The Priest:

May the Lord God remember thee in His Kingdom always, now and ever, unto ages of ages.

The Deacon :

Amen.

The Priest then says privately :

That it may be to those who partake of it for a
justification of the soul, forgiveness of sins, communion with the Holy Ghost, fulfilment of Eternal
Life, and for confidence in Thee and not for judgment
and condemnation.

We offer, moreover, unto Thee this our reasonable service for those who have departed this life in
the faith, for our forefathers, for the Fathers of the
Patriarchs, Apostles, Prophets, Preachers, Evangelists, Martyrs, Confessors, Ascetics, and for every
righteous soul made perfect in the Faith.

[Or if the Liturgy of St. Basil the Great be used :

Unite us all who partake of this one Bread and
one Cup in the Communion of the Holy Spirit, and
suffer none of us to receive of the Holy Body and
Blood of Christ to our judgment and condemnation;
but grant that we may find mercy and grace with all
Thy Saints who have been pleasing unto Thee from
the beginning of the world, our Forefathers, with the
Patriarchs, Prophets, Apostles, Preachers, Evangelists, Martyrs, Confessors, Teachers, and every just
soul departed in the Faith.]

Then shall the Deacon cense the Altar and make mention of such of the dead and of the living as he think fit.

The Priest (aloud):

Especially the most holy, immaculate, blessed, and glorious Lady, the Mother of God and Ever-Virgin Mary.

The Choir:

It is very meet to bless Thee who bore the Christ, O ever Blessed and Immaculate Mother of God. More wondrous than the Cherubim and of greater glory than the Seraphim art Thou who remaining Virgin didst give birth to God the Word. Verily, do we magnify Thee, O Mother of God. In Thee, O full of grace, all creation exults, the hierarchy of Angels and the race of men. In Thee sanctified temple, spiritual paradise, glory of virgins, of Whom God took flesh through Whom our God Who was before the world became a child. Of Thy womb he made a throne, and its dominion is more extensive than the Heavens. In Thee, O full of grace, all creation exults: glory to Thee.

On Feasts they shall, however, sing the Hymn appointed for the day.

Then shall the Priest say privately:

And St. John the Prophet, the fore-runner and

the Baptist. The Holy and venerable Apostles St. N. *(here shall he name the Saint of the day)* whom we commemorate, and all Thy Saints: For the sake of whose prayers, O God, vouchsafe to look upon us, and be not unmindful of those that rest in the hope of Resurrection to life eternal.

Here shall the Priest make remembrance of such of the living and dead as he deem fit.

For the living he shall say aloud:

For health, protection and remission of the sins of N., the servant of God.

For the dead:

For the remission and forgiveness of the soul of Thy servant N. Give it rest, O God, in a pleasant place where there is neither sorrow nor mourning. Give him rest, O our God.

Then shall the Priest continue privately:

Give them rest where they may rejoice in the Light of Thy countenance. We beseech Thee like-wise, O Lord, to call to remembrance all orthodox Bishops and those who rightly dispense the Gospel of Thy Truth, the Priests and Deacons in Christ, and all others serving in Thy Ministry. Furthermore, we offer unto Thee this one reasonable service on behalf of the whole world; of the Holy Catholic and

Apostolic Church; of those who continue in charity and holiness; of our most God-fearing Sovereign N., the Emperor of all the Russias; of all the Royal House, their Council, their Army and their Navy. Give them, O Lord, a peaceful reign that in their peace we may lead an untroubled life in all godliness and honesty.

[*But if the Liturgy of St. Basil the Great be used :*

Give them rest where they may rejoice in the light of Thy Countenance. Furthermore, we beseech Thee, O Lord, to call to remembrance Thy Holy and Apostolic Church which is spread over the face of the whole earth; and give peace unto Her Whom Thou hast purchased with the precious Blood of Thy Christ, and establish this Holy Temple that it may continue to the end of the world. Remember, O Lord, those who have offered these gifts and those for whom and by whom and on whose behalf they are offered.

Remember, O Lord, those in the Holy Church who bring forth good fruit; are rich in good works and forget not the poor; reward them with the abundant riches of the Heavenly Grace; for their earthly things give them things divine; for their temporal; eternal; for their corruptible, those that will not decay.

Remember, O Lord, those in deserts, mountains, dens, and caves of the earth. Remember, O Lord, those who live in virginity and piety, meditation and

Holy converse. Remember, O Lord, our most religious and faithful sovereign, N. Emperor of all the Russians, whom Thou hast appointed to reign over us on earth; defend him with the shield of truth; strengthen his arm and exalt his right hand, and subject unto him all barbarous nations who delight in war; grant unto him a profound and lasting peace; incline his heart toward Thy Church and toward Thy people that in his peace we may lead an untroubled life in all godliness and honesty.

Remember, O Lord, all in power and authority, and our brethren who are in his service, his army and navy, those that are good preserve in goodness, and of Thy mercy convert those that are evil.

Remember, O Lord, this congregation here present, and those who are absent with good cause; have mercy upon them and upon us according to the multitude of Thy loving kindness; fill their garners with good things, preserve their unions in peace and love, rear their infants, guide their youth, strengthen the aged, comfort the timid, collect the scattered, bring back those who have erred, and unite them all in Thy Holy Catholic and Apostolic Church. Succour those who are vexed with unclean spirits, accompany those that travel by sea or by land, protect the widow, shelter the fatherless, deliver those who are in captivity, and heal the sick.

Remember, O Lord, those who are called to judgment and those in the mines or in exile, in distress, necessity or any tribulation. Remember all who stand in need of Thy pity; those that love us, and those that hate us, and those who desire our prayers, unworthy though we be to offer them unto Thee.

Remember, O Lord our God, all Thy people, and pour upon them the abundance of Thy goodness, granting all their prayers unto Salvation. All those whom we have not remembered through ignorance or forgetfulness, or through the multiplicity of their names, do Thou Thyself call to mind, O God Who knowest, the age and name of each, even from his mother's womb. For Thou, O Lord, art the Helper of the helpless, the Hope of the hopeless, the Saviour of the tempest-tossed, the Port of the sailor, and the Physician of the sick. Be Thou all things to all men, for Thou knowest them all, their petitions, their dwellings, and their minds. Deliver, O Lord, this city and every city existing from famine, plague, earthquake, inundation, fire, sword, invasion, and Civil war.]

Then the Deacon shall turn to the Door of the Sacred Place, and, holding his Stole in three fingers, shall say:

And all men and women.

The Choir:

And all men and women.

The Priest (in a loud voice):

In the first place, remember, O Lord, our most

H

sacred Metropolitan N.; preserve him for the sake of Thy Holy Church in safety, honour, health, long life, and rightly disseminating Thy Truth.

The Deacon standing up at the door shall say:

For N., our most sacred Metropolitan, and for the most devout priest who is now offering these gifts. For the safety of our most religious Emperor N., who is God's special care, and for all men and women.

The Choir:

For all men and women.

The Priest privately:

Remember, O Lord, this city wherein we dwell, and every other city in the country, and all the faithful who in them dwell. Remember, O Lord, all who travel by sea or land, all sick persons, all they that suffer, and all who are in captivity, and their salvation.

Remember, O Lord, those who in Thy Holy Church bear good fruit, and are rich in good works, and forget not the poor. Grant unto us all Thy mercy and loving kindness.

[But if the Liturgy of St. Basil the Great be used, the Priest shall pray in a low voice:

Remember, O Lord, all orthodox bishops, who rightly disseminate the Word of Thy Truth. Remember according to the multitude of Thy mercies my unworthiness. Pardon my offences, voluntary and involuntary, nor on account of my sins withhold the force of Thy Holy Spirit from these gifts, now spread before Thee. Remember, O Lord, all Priests and Deacons in Christ, and every priestly order. And put us not to confusion who officiate at Thy Holy Altar. Visit us with Thy loving kindness, and manifest Thyself to us, O Lord, in Thy abundant mercy. Vouchsafe unto us seasonable weather, and rains for the production of fruits; and crown the year with the blessings of Thy goodness; heal the schisms within Thy Church, and quench the raging of the heathen, and put a stop to growing heresies by the power of Thy Holy Spirit. Receive us all into Thy Kingdom, making us children of light and of the day. Grant us, O Lord our God, Thy peace and Thy love for Thou it is Who bestowest all things upon us.

The Priest (in a loud voice):

And grant that we may with one mouth and one heart praise and glorify Thy great and glorious Name, Father, Son, and Holy Ghost, world without end.

The Choir:

Amen.]

The Priest, turning to the people, shall bless them in a loud voice, and say:

The blessing of the Great God and of our Saviour Jesus Christ be with you all.

The Choir:

And with Thy Spirit.

The Deacon shall then pass through the door, and, returning to his accustomed place, shall say:

Commemorating all Saints, let us again and again pray unto the Lord.

The Choir:

Lord, have mercy upon us.

The Deacon:

For the precious Gifts which are now offered and consecrated, let us pray unto the Lord.

The Choir:

Lord, have mercy upon us.

The Deacon:

Let us pray unto the Lord that our God Who loveth mankind will accept Them upon His Holy Heavenly and Spiritual Altar, for a savour of Celestial fragrance; and will send down upon us the gift of the Holy Ghost.

The Choir:

Lord, have mercy upon us.

The Deacon:

Let us pray unto the Lord that we may be delivered from all affliction, wrath, peril, and necessity.

The Choir:

Lord, have mercy upon us.

The Deacon:

Succour us, save us, have mercy upon us.

The Choir:

Lord, have mercy upon us.

The Deacon:

Let us beseech the Lord to grant us a day all perfect, holy, peaceful, and free from sin.

The Choir:

Grant this, O Lord.

The Deacon:

Let us beseech the Lord to grant us an Angel of Peace.

The Choir:

Grant this, O Lord.

The Deacon:

Let us beseech the Lord to grant pardon and remission of our transgressions.

The Choir:

Grant this, O Lord.

The Deacon:

Let us beseech the Lord to grant all things profitable to ourselves and peace to the world.

The Choir:

Grant this, O Lord.

The Deacon:

Let us beseech the Lord to grant that we may pass the remainder of our life in peace and penitence.

The Choir:

Grant this, O Lord.

The Deacon:

Let us beseech the Lord to grant a Christian ending to our life, painless, peaceful, and without blame; and a sure defence before the dread judgment seat of Christ.

The Choir:

Grant this, O Lord.

The Deacon:

Having made our petition for the unity of the Faith, and the Communion of the Holy Spirit, let us commend ourselves and one another, and our whole life unto Christ our God.

The Choir:

To Thee, O Lord.

Then shall the Priest say privately:

Unto Thee, O gracious Lord, do we commend our life and hope, and pray, beseech, and implore Thee to make us worthy to partake of the Heavenly and tremendous mysteries of this Sacred and Spiritual Table, with a pure conscience for the remission of our sins, and for the pardon of our transgressions, for the Fellowship of the Holy Ghost, the inheritance of the Kingdom of Heaven, and for confidence toward Thee, and not for judgment and condemnation.

[Or if the Liturgy of St. Basil the Great be used:

Our God, God of salvation, teach us worthily to give thanks unto Thee for the benefits Thou hast bestowed and dost bestow upon us. O God who hast received these Gifts, purify us from all defilement of flesh and of spirit, and teach us so to perfect holiness in Thy fear that we partaking of these Holy Mysteries with the testimony of a good conscience, may be partakers of the most Holy Body and Blood of Thy Christ, and that receiving Them worthily we may have Christ abiding in our hearts, and become the temple of Thy Holy Spirit. But O our God make us not guilty either in soul or body of this Thy terrible and Heavenly sacrament, by an unworthy reception of the same; but grant that to the end of our lives we may duly employ this means of sanctification as the viaticum of life eternal; and as a valid plea at the terrible judgment seat of Thy Christ, that we together with Thy Saints, who have pleased Thee from the beginning of the world, may be partakers in those good things which Thou hast prepared for them that love Thee, O Lord.]

The Priest (in a loud voice):

And grant, O Lord, that we may boldly and without condemnation persevere to call upon Thee our Heavenly Father, and say:

Here the Deacon shall bind his Stole about him crosswise.

The People :

"Our Father which art in Heaven, Hallowed be
Thy Name, Thy Kingdom come, Thy will be done in
earth as it is in Heaven.   Give us this day our daily
bread ; And forgive us our trespasses, as we forgive
them that trespass against us ; And lead us not into
temptation ; But deliver us from evil.

The Priest (in a loud voice):

For Thine is the Kingdom, the power, and the
glory, Father, Son and Holy Ghost, world without
end.

The Choir :

Amen.

The Priest :

Peace be with you all.

The Choir :

And with Thy Spirit.

The Deacon :

Let us bow our heads unto the Lord.

The Choir:

To Thee, O Lord.

The Priest, in a bowing posture, says privately:

We give thanks to Thee, O invisible King, Who of Thine infinite power hast made all things, and of the plentitude of Thy mercy hast called all things from nothing into being. Look down from Heaven, O Lord, upon those who bow their heads to Thee, for they have not bowed down to flesh and blood, but to Thee a great and Terrible God. Bestow, therefore, O Lord, a benefit from these mysteries according to our several necessities. Watch over those who travel by sea or by land, and heal all who are diseased Thou who art the Physician of our Souls and of our Bodies.

[Or if the Liturgy of St. Basil the Great be used:

O, Almighty Lord, Father of mercies, and God of all comfort, bless, sanctify, guard, strengthen, and confirm those who have bowed their heads to Thee; turn them from evil deeds and unite them in every good work. And grant that they may without condemnation partake in these Immaculate and Life giving Mysteries, unto the remission of their sins and the Communion of the Holy Spirit.]

Then the Priest (in a loud voice):

Through the grace and mercy and loving kindness of Thine Only Begotten Son with Whom together with the Holy Good and Life-giving Spirit, Thou art blessed, now henceforth and for ever.

The Choir:

Amen.

The Priest privately:

From the habitation of Thy dwelling, and the Throne of glory of Thy Kingdom, draw near and sanctify us, O Lord Jesus Christ our God, Who sittest on high with the Father, and art Invisibly present with us. And deign with Thine Own mighty hand to impart to us Thine Immaculate Body and Thy precious Blood, and through us to all Thy people.

Then the Priest bows in adoration, and the Deacon stands before the Holy Door, and both shall say privately:

O God, be merciful to me a sinner. *(Thrice.)*

And the Deacon, when he sees the Priest stretching out his hands and touching the Holy Bread in the act of making the Oblation, shall say in a loud voice:

Let us attend.

The Holy Door is now closed and the Curtain is drawn.

And the Priest, elevating the Holy Bread, shall say aloud:

Holy Things unto the Holy.

The Choir:

One only is Holy, one only is the Lord Jesus Christ in the glory of God the Father.   Amen.

Then the Choir shall chant:

Praise ye the Lord from Heaven, Praise Him in the height.   Alleluia.

Or the Antiphon appointed of the day or of the Saint whose Feast is celebrated.

Then the Deacon shall enter the Sanctuary, and girding himself with the Stole in the form of a Cross, and standing at the right hand of the Priest, shall say:

Break, Master the Holy Bread.

Then the Priest carefully and reverently shall break it into four parts, and say:

Broken and divided is the Lamb of God, Son of the Father.   Divided but not diminished, distributed but not consumed, sanctifying those who partake.

Then he takes one piece of the Holy Bread and holds it in his hand, and the Deacon, pointing with the Stole to the Holy Cup, shall say:

Fill, Master, the Holy Cup.

Then the Priest shall say:

The fulness of faith is of the Holy Ghost.

And making the sign of the Cross puts it into the Holy Cup.

The Deacon:

Amen.

And taking warm water, he says to the Priest:

Bless, Master, this Holy Water.

And the Priest shall bless it, saying:

Blessed be the fervour of Thy Saints now henceforth and for evermore.   Amen.

Then the Deacon shall pour it in the form of a Cross into the Holy Cup, saying:

The fervour of faith and of the Holy Ghost. Amen.   *(Thrice.)*

Then setting down the vessel of warm water, he shall stand at a little distance, and the Priest shall say:

Deacon, draw near.

The Deacon shall approach, and bowing reverently makes his confession and desires forgiveness, and having kissed the Altar shall say:

Lo! I draw near unto the King Immortal and to God. Make me partaker, O Master, of the Precious and Holy Blood of our Lord God our Saviour Jesus Christ.

And the Priest shall give him a portion, and say:

N. the Holy Deacon is made partaker of the Precious, Holy, and Immaculate Body of our Lord, God, our Saviour Jesus Christ for the remission of sins and eternal life.

The Priest and the Deacon then withdraw behind the Holy Altar, and both shall say:

I believe, O Lord, and confess that Thou art in very truth Christ the Son of the Living God Who didst come into the world to save sinners of whom I am chief.

Then the Priest makes an obeisance to the Deacon and then to the People, and shall say:

Forgive me, fathers and brethren.

And kissing the Altar he continues:

Lo, I draw near unto the King Immortal and to God. I, N. priest do partake of the Precious and

Immaculate Body of our Lord and God our Saviour
Jesus Christ unto the remission of my sins, and unto
life eternal.

*Then he shall take a portion of the Holy Bread, and bow-
ing low over the Altar and gazing devoutly upon the Holy
Body, shall say privately:*

I believe, O Lord, and confess that Thou art in
very truth Christ the Son of the Living God Who didst
come into the world to save sinners of whom I am
chief. And I believe that this is of a truth Thine
Immaculate Body and this Thy Precious Blood.
And I beseech Thee to have mercy upon me and to
forgive my transgressions voluntary and involuntary,
of word or deed, and vouchsafe that I may partake
without condemnation of Thy pure Mysteries unto
the remission of my sins and unto life eternal.

O, Son of God, receive me as a partaker of Thy
Mystical Supper. For not as a secret enemy do I
approach, not with the kiss of Judas, but as the thief,
will confess Thee. Remember me, O Lord, in Thy
Kingdom. I am not worthy, Lord, that Thou
shouldst come unto me, but as Thou wast content to
lodge in the stable of brute beasts, and in the house
of Simon the leper, and didst receive the harlot, a
sinner like unto me, vouchsafe in a like measure to
enter into the stable of my brutish soul, my defiled
body, dead in sin and spiritually leprous. And in as
much as Thou didst not disdain the foul mouth of the

harlot, when she kissed Thine unpolluted feet, disdain not me a sinner, O Lord my God, but make me worthy to partake of Thy Most Holy Body and Blood.

And let not this participation in Thy Holy Mysteries be a judgment upon me unto condemnation, O Lord, but unto the healing of my soul and body. For Thine is the Kingdom, the power and the glory, now henceforth, and unto ages of ages. Amen.

Then he shall partake of the Holy Blood thrice, saying:

(First). The Precious and Holy Blood of our Lord God and Saviour Jesus Christ is imparted unto me the Priest N. servant of God unto the remission of my sins unto life eternal.

In the name of the Father.

(Second). The Precious and Holy Blood of our Lord God and Saviour Jesus Christ is imparted unto me, the Priest N., servant of God, unto the remission of my sins and unto life eternal.

In the name of the Son.

(Third). The Precious and Holy Blood of our Lord God and Saviour Jesus Christ is imparted unto me, the Priest N., servant of God, unto the remission of my sins and unto life eternal.

And of the Holy Ghost.

And after he has received he shall reverently wipe the Holy Cup and his own lips with the Veil, saying:

Lo, this has touched my lips, and shall take

away mine iniquities, and shall purge me from my sins from this time forth and for evermore. Amen.

And still holding the Cup in his hand, he shall call the Deacon, saying:

Deacon, draw near.

And the Deacon shall approach, and, making reverence, shall say:

Behold, I draw near to the Immortal King.   I believe, O Lord, and confess that Thou art in very truth Christ, the Son of the Living God, who didst come into the world to save sinners of whom I am chief.

And the Priest, giving him the Cup, shall say:

Thou O N. deacon, servant of God, receive this, the Precious and Holy Body and Blood of our Lord and Saviour Jesus Christ, for the remission of sins and for eternal life.

And the Deacon, having received, the Priest shall say:

Lo, this has touched Thy lips, and shall take away thine iniquities, purge thy sins from this time forth and for evermore. Amen.

ı

If there be any who desire to partake of the Holy Mysteries the Priest shall divide the remaining portions of the Holy Body into small Particles sufficient for all, and the Deacon, setting the Paten upon the Holy Cup, shall say this Hymn in a loud voice:

In that we have beheld the resurrection of Christ, let us bow down before the Holy Lord Jesus, Who alone is sinless. We adore Thy Cross, O Christ, and glorify and praise Thy Holy Resurrection. For Thou art our God, and we know none but Thee, we call upon Thy Name, O come all ye faithful, let us acclaim Christ's Holy Resurrection; for He hath endured the Cross, and by death has conquered Death. Rejoice, O new Jerusalem, for the glory of God sheds its lustre upon Thee. Lift up your voices, O Sion, and be glad. And do Thou, O Pure Mother of God, rejoice in the Resurrection of Him Whom Thou hast borne. O Christ great and most Holy Passover, Wisdom, Word, and Power of God, vouchsafe that we may more perfectly partake of Thee in the eternal days of Thy Kingdom.

Then he shall reverently wipe all the Particles into the Cup, and say:

Wash away, O Lord, the sins of all who are here commemorated by Thy Precious Blood, through the prayers of Thy Saints.

And he shall cover the Cup with the Veil, and the Holy Paten with the Star, Cover and the Veil. Then the Priest shall say in a low voice:

We give thanks unto Thee, O Lord, Who lovest mankind, Thou benefactor of our souls and bodies, for that Thou hast vouchsafed this day to feed us with Thy Heavenly Mysteries, guide our path aright, establish us all in Thy fear, guard our lives, make sure our steps through the prayers and supplications of the glorious Mother of God and Ever Virgin Mary and of all Thy Saints.

[Or if the Liturgy of St. Basil the Great be used:

We give thanks unto Thee, O Lord our God, for our participation in Thy Holy, Immaculate, Eternal, and Heavenly Mysteries which Thou hast given unto us for the welfare and sanctification and healing of our souls and bodies. Do Thou, the same, O Lord, grant that the communion of the Holy Body and Blood of Thy Christ may be for us unto faith that maketh not ashamed, unto love unfeigned, unto fulness of wisdom, unto healing of soul and body, unto the defeat of every adversary, unto the fulfilment of all Thy commandments, and unto an acceptable defence at the dread judgment seat of Thy Christ.]

Then the Holy Door is opened, and the Deacon, making a reverence, shall stand at the entrance, and taking from the Priest the Cup, and elevating it, shall say:

Draw near in the fear of God and in faith.

The Choir:

Blessed is he that cometh in the name of the Lord. The Lord is God, and hath revealed Himself unto us.

At Easter he shall add:

Christ is risen from the dead, conquering death by death, and bestowing life upon those who lie in the grave.

Then those who desire to communicate shall draw near singly, do reverence with their hands crossed on their breast, and the Priest having said aloud the Prayer:

I believe, O Lord, and I confess, etc.   (See page 127.)

Shall administer the Holy Sacrament unto them, and as he communicateth each one he shall say:

The servant of God N. partaketh of the Precious and Holy Body and Blood of our Lord God and Saviour Jesus Christ unto the remission of his sins and unto life eternal.

And as each person is communicated the Choir shall sing:

Receive ye the Body of Christ; drink ye of the Fountain of Life.

Then the Communicant's mouth shall be wiped with the Veil, and having kissed the Cup and made reverence, he shall go aside and receive the Antidoron,[1] and the Choir shall sing:

Alleluia, Alleluia, Alleluia.

Then shall the Priest set the Cup upon the Altar and bless the people, saying:

O Lord, save Thy people, and bless Thine inheritance.

The Choir:

We have beheld the light of Truth, we have received the Heavenly Spirit; we have found the True Faith. Let us bow down and worship the undivided Trinity in which is our salvation.

At Eastertide:

Christ is risen from the dead, conquering Death

---

1 The Antidoron is the Bread which has been offered for the service of the Altar, but has not been needed for consecration ; and resembles the *pain bénit* distributed in many French churches. It is not unusual in Russia for Monks to take no other food during Lent.

by death; and bestowing life upon those who lie in the grave.

Then the Priest and the Deacon shall turn toward the Altar, and the Priest shall cense it, saying in a loud voice:

Be Thou exalted in Heaven and Thy glory above all the earth.

The Priest taking the Holy Paten shall set it upon the head of the Deacon, and the Deacon going to the place of ablution shall set it therein. The Priest having done reverence shall take the Holy Cup, and looking upon the people shall say aloud:

Blessed is our God. *(And then raising his voice.)* Always now and ever, unto ages of ages.

The Choir:

Amen. Let our mouths be filled with Thy praise, O Lord, that we may extol Thy glory; for Thou hast designed to make us participants in Thy Holy, Divine, Eternal, and Quickening Mysteries. Sanctify us so that all the day long we may meditate upon Thy wondrous goodness.

At Eastertide the following is added:

Christ is risen from the dead, conquering Death by death.

*Then the Deacon, coming forth through the North Door
and standing in his accustomed place, shall say:*

Having received the Holy, Divine, Pure, Eternal,
Quickening and Terrible Mysteries of Christ, let us
O believers give the due thanks unto the Lord.

The Choir:

Lord, have mercy.

The Deacon:

Assist, preserve, pity, and keep us, O God, by
Thy Grace.

The Choir:

Lord, have mercy.

The Deacon:

Beseeching that the whole day may be perfect,
holy, peaceful, and without sin, let us commend ourselves and each other, and all our life unto Christ our
God.

The Choir:

To Thee, O Lord.

Then the Priest, folding the Corporal, shall make over it with the Book of the Gospels the sign of the Cross, and say in a loud voice:

For Thou art our sanctification to Thee do we ascribe glory and to the Son, and to the Holy Ghost, now and ever world without end.

The Choir:

Amen.

The Priest:

Let us depart in peace.

The Deacon:

Let us pray unto the Lord.

The Choir:

Lord, have mercy.

Then the Priest cometh forth, and standing at the foot of the Tribune says:

O Lord, Who blessest them that bless Thee and sanctifieth them that trust in Thee. Save Thy people and bless their inheritance. Preserve the fulness of Thy Church, sanctify them that love the beauty of Thine House; give them a glorious reward through Thy Divine power, and forsake us not who put our trust in Thee. Give peace to Thy world, to Thy churches, to the priests, to our most God-fearing Sovereign N., the Emperor of all the Russias, to the Army and Navy, and to all Thy people. For every good gift and every perfect gift is from above, and cometh from Thee, the Father of Light. And to Thee we ascribe glory and thanksgiving and adoration Father, Son and Holy Ghost now and ever world without end.

The Choir:

Amen. Blessed be the Name of the Lord henceforth and for ever. *(Thrice.)*

The Deacon, holding his Stole in his hand, shall stand at the right side of the image-screen before the Holy Ikon of our Lord Christ until the conclusion of the Prayer before the Tribune. And after this has been said, the Priest, entering the Holy Door and going to the Table of Oblation, shall say the following secretly:

Thou, O Christ our God, who art Thyself the fulness of the Law and the Prophets, and didst accomplish all the dispensations of Thy Father: fill our hearts with joy and gladness, now and evermore world without end.

The Reader shall then read Psalm xxxiv.

I will alway give thanks unto the Lord: His praise shall ever be in my mouth.

My soul shall make her boast in the Lord: the humble shall hear thereof, and be glad.

O praise the Lord with me: and let us magnify His Name together.

I sought the Lord, and He heard me: yea, He delivered me out of all my fear.

They had an eye unto Him, and were lightened, and their faces were not ashamed.

Lo, the poor crieth, and the Lord heareth him: yea, and saveth him out of all his troubles.

The Angel of the Lord tarrieth round about them that fear Him : and delivereth them

O taste, and see, how gracious the Lord is: blessed is the man that trusteth in Him.

O fear the Lord, ye, that are His saints: for they that fear Him lack nothing.

The lions do lack, and suffer hunger: but they who seek the Lord shall want no manner of thing that is good.

Come, ye children, and hearken unto me: I will teach you the fear of the Lord.

What man is he that lusteth to live: and would fain see good days?

Keep thy tongue from evil: and thy lips, that they speak no guile.

Eschew evil, and do good: seek peace, and ensue it.

The eyes of the Lord are over the righteous: and His ears are open unto their prayers.

The countenance of the Lord is against them that

do evil: to root out the remembrance of them from the earth.

The righteous cry, and the Lord heareth them: and delivereth them out of all their troubles.

The Lord is nigh unto them that are of a contrite heart: and will save such as be of an humble spirit.

Great are the troubles of the righteous: but the Lord delivereth him out of all.

He keepeth all his bones: so that not one of them are broken.

But misfortune shall slay the ungodly: and they that hate the righteous shall be desolate.

The Lord delivereth the souls of His servants: and all they that put their trust in Him shall not be destitute.

And at Eastertide he shall add:

Christ is risen from the dead, conquering Death by death, and giving life to them that lie in the grave.

While the Psalm is being read the Deacon shall consume the Holy Elements so that not the smallest Particle shall fall out or be left.

Then the Priest shall say:

The blessing of the Lord through His grace and love toward mankind be upon you now and ever, unto ages of ages.

The Choir:

Amen.

The Priest:

Glory to Thee, O Christ our God.   Glory to Thee.

The Choir:

Glory be to the Father and to the Son and to the Holy Ghost now and ever, world without end. Lord, have mercy. *(Thrice.)*

The Deacon:

Bless, Master. *(At Eastertide he adds).*

Christ is risen from the dead, conquering Death by death, and giving life to them that lie in the grave.

The Priest shall then say the Benediction:

May He who rose from the dead, Christ our True God, through the intercession of His undefiled Mother and of the august powers of Heaven *(and of the Saint of the day)* of the Holy Glorious and most laudable Apostles, of our Fathers amongst the Saints *(John Chrysostom or St. Basil according to the Liturgy used)* of the Holy and righteous ancestors of God, Joachim and Anna, and of all the Saints, have mercy upon us and save us: for He is good and loveth mankind.

The Priest shall then hold the Cross for the people to kiss, and shall distribute the Antidoron, after which he shall withdraw to the Sanctuary, and the Holy Door is closed.

He shall then recite the Post Communion Prayer.

The Priest:

Glory to Thee, O God. *(Thrice.)* I thank Thee, O Lord my God, that Thou hast not requited me a sinner, but hast deemed me worthy to partake in Thy Holy Mysteries. I thank Thee that Thou hast graciously permitted me, unworthy though I be, to receive Thy pure and Heavenly Gifts. O Master Who loved mankind, and Who for our sake didst die and rise again, and hast graciously bestowed upon us Thy Terrible and Life-giving Sacrament for the blessing and sanctification of our souls and bodies, grant that they may effectually heal my soul and avert all evil from it so that the eyes of my heart may be enlightened, making for the peace of my spiritual powers for faith invisible, for love unfeigned, increasing Thy Divine Grace, and assuring the attainment of Thy Kingdom; that by Thee preserved in Thy Holiness, I may bear in mind the bounteousness of Thy grace, and live not unto myself but unto Thee our Lord and benefactor. So that this life ended in the hope of life eternal, I may come into that everlasting rest where the voices of those who keep high festival shall never cease, and where the beatitude of those who behold the

ineffable beauty of Thy countenance is infinite. For
Thou art the True Desire and Unutterable good of
those who love Thee, O Christ our God, and all
created beings should render praises to Thee for all
eternity. Amen.

[*Or if the Liturgy of St. Basil be used:*

O Lord Christ God, King of the Ages, and Creator
of all mankind, I thank thee for all the benefits Thou
hast conferred upon me, and for the communion of
Thy most pure and quickening Mysteries. I entreat
Thee, O Perfect One Who lovest mankind, to cherish
me in Thy tabernacle and under the shadow of Thy
wings. And grant that with a clear conscience, even
at my last breath, I may worthily participate of Thy
Holy Sacrament, for the remission of my sins, and
unto life eternal. For Thou art the Bread of Life, the
Fountain of all Holiness, the Giver of all good; and
unto Thee do we ascribe glory, with the Father, Son,
and Holy Ghost, now and ever, world without end.
Amen.]

*The Priest and the Deacon then wash their hands in the
place appointed, and having done reverence, the Priest
pronounces the Dismissory Prayer of St. Chrysostom.*

The Grace of Thy lips shining forth like a beacon
light hath illumined the world, enriched the universe
with the treasure of liberality, and hath manifested
to us the height of humility; but as Thou instructest

us by Thy words, O Father John Chrysostom, so also intercede thou for us with Christ our God that our souls may be saved.

Lord, have mercy upon us. *(Twelve times.)*

Glory be to the Father and to the Son and to the Holy Ghost. As it was in beginning, now and ever shall be world without end. Amen.

Then they shall go their way in Peace.

Printed in Great Britain
by Amazon